RELIGIONS
OF THE WORLD

EVERYDAY HANDBOOKS

Estimated Population of the World by Major Religious Beliefs

Sect	Americas	Eurasia	Africa & Oceania	Total
Roman Catholic	242,361,000	281,475,000	26,514,000	550,350,000
Orthodox Christian	2,916,500	129,172,000	4,945,000	137,033,500
Protestant	78,194,000	123,056,000	15,699,000	216,949,000
Taoist & Confucian	213,000	350,062,000	68,700	350,343,700
Hindu	336,800	334,708,000	757,500	335,802,300
Islam	393,000	344,450,000	88,897,000	433,740,000
Buddhist	300,000	153,010,000		153,310,000
Primitive	1,050,000	45,000,000	75,100,000	121,150,000
Shinto		51,000,000		51,000,000
Jewish	6,454,450	5,727,100	611,250	12,792,800
Zoroastrian		140,000		140,000
Grand Total	332,217,750	1,817,800,100	212,592,450	2,362,611,300

Key to Symbols: † Christianity; ☾ Islam; ✡ Judaism; ☯ Confucianism; 卍 Primitive.

RELIGIONS
OF THE WORLD

by Gerald L. Berry

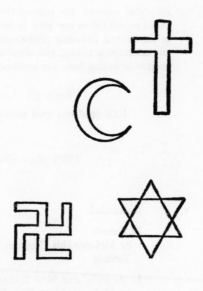

BARNES & NOBLE, Inc. · New York
Booksellers · Publishers · Since 1873

©

Copyright 1947, 1956

By Barnes & Noble, Inc.

Reprinted, 1971

L.C. catalogue card number: 56–12163

ISBN 389 00284 4

Distributed

In Canada
by McGraw-Hill Company of Canada Ltd., Toronto

In Australia and New Zealand
by Hicks, Smith & Sons Pty. Ltd., Sydney and Wellington

In the United Kingdom, Europe, and South Africa
by Chapman & Hall Ltd., London

Manufactured in the United States of America

Table of Contents

Preface

THIS little book is written by a teacher both as a source of information for the interested layman and as a handy reference for teachers and students. There is no attempt to interpret the greater religions which go to make up this "mosaic," nor is there any attempt to prognosticate the place in a new world order which any of them may occupy. My purpose is to promote good will and better understanding among peoples of diverse beliefs. I have tried to give some idea of the origin, growth, and extent of dissemination of the leading beliefs of the world, both extinct and extant. My thanks must be given to the librarians in the several public libraries in Alberta and to others who have assisted in various ways. Statistics have been carefully checked and should prove reliable, but for errors I am solely responsible.

G. L. B.

Faculty of Education
Edmonton, Alberta

Chapter I

In the Beginning—The Religion of Primitive Man

RELIGION is found in the field of the supernormal, and may be defined as a link between the finite and the infinite or as a grasping by man toward something beyond himself which gives him a reason for being. If we include all those acts, ceremonies, observances, and eccentricities of behaviour by which any group choose to believe they effect a relationship with certain external unseen beings or forces, we may assume that religion has been common to all men from earliest times. To be a truly religious belief, a belief must have an element of personal relationship, and often it involves some element of prayer, which may, however, take the form of a ceremonial dance, symbolic chant, or ritual song.

Because it is a customary social way of facing a crisis, all religion is inherently conservative and averse to change. Even today we find established churches to be among our most conservative elements. The crises which early man had to face were the basic crises of life—birth, puberty, marriage, hunger, sickness, pestilence, harvest, war, and death—and around these crises his religion was built. Later in this book we shall find that these same basic crises were the origin or fountainhead of our modern sacraments.

Religion had its birth in the fears of early man. Among most of the earliest primitives there were two kinds of spirits only—hostile spirits and neutral ones. Only later came a belief in good or helpful forces, and the idea of "God." To hide from evil spirits seemed a sensible thing to do. Mourning clothes are found very early in the history of man, and it is quite possible that they were originally used as a disguise to hide one from the spirits of the dead, since all such were considered evil. Later it was believed that spirits could be

1

made friendly through the performance of certain ritual, the observance of a fetish, or through the kindly offices of a shaman or "medicine man."

It is only a step from fetish (the use of some charm or luck symbol, such as the swastika) to the setting up of an idol or totem. The next step is to house the idol, and the first church appeared at such a stage. The medicine man became an idol-tender, or priest. To maintain his power, the priest built up a complicated ritual which only he and a chosen few could properly perform. To them there were many ways of going wrong but only one way of going right. One should compare in this regard the New Testament, Matt. 7:13-14: "Wide is the gate and broad is the way that leadeth to destruction" but "strait is the gate and narrow is the way that leadeth unto life."

But long before man had advanced to any of these refinements which mark a cultural religion, he had religious belief. This was at first based in natural objects, visible but intangible—the shadow which stayed by one's side, dreams, the breath on a cold day. Then came a belief in spirits recognizable to other senses than sight—the sighing of the wind, the whispering of leaves, the voice of running water. Together with these spirits, primitive man believed that inanimate objects possessed of virtue also possessed spirits—for example, the bow or spear-thrower, which could throw a missile farther, more accurately, and with greater force than could be achieved by man's arm alone.

The importance of this early religion should not be under estimated. It had the same efficacy as have some higher forms. It required faith, and faith restored self-confidence, which in turn made the seemingly hopeless possible of attainment.

As soon as the fetish became a totem or an idol, gifts to it were obviously in order. These gifts were the origin of sacrifice. Things most precious to man were thought to be almost precious to the god; hence prized cereals, drinks, animals of the chase, and even life itself became the common subjects of sacrifice. With increasing complication of the sacrificial rites, a priest or priest class became necessary, and the shaman was obviously the one to be chosen for the position. He—or she—was originally an intellectual leader who maintained headship by exhortation, warnings, mollification of spirits, interpretations of dreams and omens, forecasts of weather, and similar holds. Now he could increase his power by use of a complicated ritual, not always understandable to the common or "lay" man.

A further addition to his power came through the new religio-science of *tabu*—the thing forbidden. He taught that besides the god there were still many evil spirits extant which should be avoided, either because of harm which they would do or because contact with them might anger the god. Examples of tabu are found among all peoples—aversion to the flesh of some animals as food, to marriage with a close relative, to incest, murder, cursing of one's father, kindling a fire on a holy day, touching a corpse, having contact with a woman during certain times, and eating at certain periods. Many tabus still survive today as superstitions; many others as part of our mores or folkways; and still others for scientific, medical, or moral reasons. They were often a primitive means of gaining a socially desirable end.

Some peoples are still found with religion based on tabu. It is noticeable among them that there are two kinds of tabu religion, one positive, the other negative. The former is found to be the most efficacious in maintaining strict adherence to ritual. The Todas of India have a negative-type tabu religion, based on the changing of unedible buffalo milk into edible butter and buttermilk. Originally, no doubt, the tabu maintained strict cleanliness and uniform product by stating things which were not to be done by the priest in the manufacture. Today the rituals are performed in a careless and slovenly manner. Sooner or later such peoples find that commission of a breach of tabu does not bring catastrophe in its wake, and this leads to carelessness. An example of a positive-type tabu religion is found in Australia among the Arunta tribes. It deals largely with initiatory ceremonies of young men at puberty, and really amounts to their "education"—a passing on of the knowledge and customs of the tribe from the old men to the young. Here the ceremonies are much more carefully observed because some good can be seen to be derived from them.

Civilized man is by no means free from the influence of tabu. Note the observance of the "Thou shalt nots" of the

Ten Commandments of Moses by the Jews; the Jewish aversion to pork; the keeping of Lent in some Christian churches; the refusal to eat flesh of any kind by some sects; the celibacy of the Roman Catholic priesthood; the ablutions before prayers by the Mohammedan; the kneeling for prayer in many religions. The list could be extended indefinitely.

Ideas of religion change as man's type of civilization changes. Thus we find corresponding differences in the beliefs and rituals as man progresses from hunting to pastoral to agricultural stages in social advance. Much of the old magic rites remains, but it is linked more definitely with specific things in the way of life.

We find the seasons and seedtime and harvest the main interest of the farmer, and his festivals were connected with these events. At seedtime most primitives had a festival which was essentially lewd and sexual. The ritual was sometimes carried out by the priest only, sometimes by all males, sometimes by the whole populace. We find the use of the phallic symbol highly developed, the delivering up of virgins to the priesthood, and sex orgies by the whole populace in the planted fields. The object of this festival was undoubtedly to demonstrate to the gods the method of reproduction, thus ensuring plentiful crops and fruitful herds and flocks.

The harvest festival among farmer folk was one primarily of thanksgiving, and so the rites were usually sacrificial in nature. This "offering of the first fruits" included cereal sacrifices for abundant crops, animal sacrifices for herds and flocks, and human sacrifice for good health and preservation of the tribe. Only later was human sacrifice associated with seedtime, when it was usually symbolical of the death and resurrection of a saviour god.

To the nomads, on the other hand, the stars and sun (used to reckon time and direction) were more important and became the special objects of veneration. Since they were a wandering people, they had no permanent temples. Since their preservation depended most upon good leadership, the medicine man was of little importance to them, and therefore we find a priesthood nonexistent with many of these people. Sacrifice with them was rarely human, and they were the first groups to substitute inanimate effigies or dummies for animals in sacrifice—perhaps because of their poverty.

The main events in life also called for festivals. Birth called for many observances. Circumcision was commonly practiced, and still is among certain groups. The *couvade* was a curious custom commonly practiced—the father must spend in bed the period immediately following the birth of the child. A form of baptism of infants was not unknown. Puberty marked the coming to manhood and was usually celebrated with initiatory rites, sometimes by tattooing. There is a survival in the Christian ceremony of confirmation. Marriage also was a religious occasion, and many moderns still insist that a church ceremony is necessary for proper nuptials. Death marked the end of life, and many burial rites developed. We know that very early a belief in future life developed because early peoples buried all the implements of use with a man, and even some of the comforts. Mummification and mound or pyramid building are found among some. Others would not bury the dead but left the corpse exposed to the air and birds of prey, thinking that the body was the prison house of the soul which could not escape until complete destruction of the corpse. Cremation was not common with primitive people.

A changed attitude toward the gods is found, too, as man becomes more civilized. There is a definite tendency to persuade the gods to do man's will instead of trying to force them. The priest increased in importance as a result.

One of the best examples of early sun or fire worshippers is the Celts. A particular object of veneration with them was the mistletoe, because it grew between earth and sky with no visible roots in the soil. The oak was respected because it supported the mistletoe, and the places of worship therefore became first, groves of oak, and secondly, circles of stones representative of a grove. Best known of these is Stonehenge, England.

Stonehenge is the most imposing stone monument in Britain—indeed in the whole world—surviving from ancient times. Now partially in ruins, there is still sufficient of it left to make reconstruction possible. The outer work was an earthen rampart, circular in form and opening toward the northeast, about three hundred feet in diameter, with a large "slaughter stone" about twenty feet long at the opening. Within this, a circle of upright stones marks out a ring about one hundred feet in diameter. There are thirty of these stones, each about sixteen feet high, placed about three and a half feet apart. A continuous capstone, mortised and dovetailed, is supported by this ring. Within this there is another circle, concentric with the first, composed of smaller stones about six feet high and carrying no capstones. Inside these two circles there are two concentric horseshoe-shaped arcs. The first is composed of five trilithons —each made up of two uprights and a capstone. The central trilithon had uprights, each twenty-one and a half feet high, surmounted by a capstone fifteen feet long and three and a half feet high. Inside this horseshoe is a smaller one composed of nineteen stones with no capstones. Near the base of this was placed the altar stone, now in two fragments, but originally about sixteen feet long. All labor was hand done, including the transport of some of the stones perhaps as far as two hundred miles from early quarries. Some regard the form as having been made to mark the rise of the midsummer sun, and set the date circa 1700 B.C., but recent excavation indicates a much earlier date, probably in the late Neolithic period prior to the use of metal tools. Stonehenge since 1918 has been a national monument, having been presented to the British government by the owner at that time.

The Celts had both priests and priestesses. The former, called *Druids* or "Wise Ones," had special rites to perform, usually connected with sacrifice. Human sacrifices seem to have been common. Rites of the priestesses were of a sexual nature. All festivals were marked with great bonfires and sex orgies in the fields. The three main festivals were Beltane on the eve of May 1st, Lugnasad on June 24 and Samhain on October 31st. Samhain was regarded as the day when the spirits of the dead could return to forgather with the living. It survives in our Hallowe'en, or All Saints' Day. Beltane survives in our Maypole dances and May-day celebrations, and Lugnasad in Midsummer Night and St. John's Day festivals.

As tribes fused, so gods were fused. Thus the chief gods

(usually with similar attributes) became composites, and often had composite names, e.g., Bel-Marduk, of whom more later. Thus multiplication of names permitted more peaceful fusion of tribes and of religions. We see the tendency down to the time of Christ, the Saviour, the Son of God, the Logos, the Lamb, etc.—all terms added to deity to make it more understandable to the people. These gods became divine leaders. In a later period they were thought to exact penalties for undetected crimes, crime thus becoming a "sin." The explanation of the fact that no visible punishment was visited on the criminal led to the belief in a future life of punishments. Only long after this belief developed, did the idea of a future life of rewards occur to man. With this stage, we find religion to be the salvation of morals just as ancestor worship later became the salvation of society.

Chapter II

Worship in Egypt and the Middle East

EGYPT

IN Egypt we find a curious mixture of ancestor worship, animal and nature worship, totemism, sun worship, and a high type of monotheistic belief. It may be because of admixture of peoples or fusion of tribes, or it may be because old forms were retained while new ones were added. Each dynasty as it came to power tended to set up its own family deity as the chief god of the people, adding to it all the attributes of other main deities. For these reasons we find the same god at different periods of Egyptian history with changed attributes. Osiris, for example, was successively god of the Nile, a life-giver, a sun-god, god of justice and love, and finally a resurrected god who ruled in the afterlife.

The two main religions of the earliest period seem to have been animal worship and ancestor worship. In the former, animals were credited with extraordinary powers, either real or imagined, such as strength, wisdom, fertility, or foresight. These animal spirits could influence a man for good or evil, but, although idolized and worshipped, seem to have had little moral significance in the lives of the people. Totemism was a natural growth in animal worship. The symbols at first were the animals themselves, later human bodies with animal heads. Greatest of these animal deities was Amon, the ram.

Ancestor worship became mixed very early with worship of the great natural forces around the people—the sun, the moon, the Nile River. The greatest deities were Re, the sun-god; Osiris, god of the Nile; Isis, his sister and also his wife; Horus, their son; Chnum, the architect, god of cataracts; Dhuti, a composite god of the moon, writing, and time, especially sacred to the priests; and Set, the god of

8

darkness. The most sacred text was the Book of the Dead or Book of the Gates, a collection of magic formulae and spells making possible the passage of the soul from earth to the judgment hall of Osiris. Re, originally the greatest of these deities, had as his symbols the winged sun disk and the pyramid.

Osiris is usually represented as a mummy from whose body sprouted cereals. He rapidly supplanted Re as chief god, even taking to himself the attributes of a sun-god. He represented imperishable life as vegetation grew and died and grew again with the changing seasons. People recognized him as a god of both the living and the dead. Later he was acclaimed as king and judge in the next world. The most popular legend about Osiris is one of a resurrected god. He was killed by Set, the god of darkness. Isis, his wife, sought him, weeping so copiously that the Nile overflowed its banks. She at last found the body and gave it burial, but not a careful burial. While she was absent tending the young Horus, Set exhumed the body, dismembered the corpse, and scattered the parts throughout the land. Isis, stricken because of her careless attention previously, carefully sought for and found each part, then gave the whole a proper burial. Osiris was then resurrected and went to live on high. This myth explained the annual cycle of seasons and the overflow of the Nile River so important and vital to agricultural Egypt. Osiris became the first of a long line of resurrected deities— Tammuz, Mithras, Balder, Christ. Every spring the life of Osiris was re-enacted at Abydos in a stirring passion play, dating back to the eighteenth or nineteenth century before Christ. This play is the earliest record in history of drama.

Ancestor worship had another important attribute in its inordinate attention to complicated burial rites. Osiris worship strengthened the belief in immortality. At first only the kings and leaders were immortal, and we find great pyramid tombs to house them; but later all men and even the sacred animals were thought to have immortality. To preserve the corpse as a home for the soul, so that it would not wander forlornly about the earth, mummification was practiced. The entrails and the heart were removed from the corpse, which was then steeped in spices and preservatives to prevent decay. Among the richer classes, it was then swathed in linen

bandages and given an elaborate burial. The dead led a sort
of double life, and had to be supplied with food, implements, and most particularly the *Book of the Dead*. This
was a papyrus roll, sometimes as much as ninety feet long,
filled with charms, pictures, and formulae. This was essential to a soul's journey from the earth to the judgment hall
of Osiris. Once in the judgment hall, the soul was judged
strictly according to its merit and morality in life, but the
Egyptian never quite reached the belief that virtue alone
would get one into heaven. Osiris is often pictured as weigh-
ing a soul in the balances against a feather, the symbol of
truth and justice. His worship had some moral significance,
as seen in this extract from the "Repudiation of Sins" before the great judgment throne—a forerunner of the Ten
Commandments of Moses:

Hail to thee, Great God, Lord of Truth and Justice—I have
not committed iniquity against men. I have not oppressed the
poor. I have not caused the slave to be ill-treated of his master.
I have not pulled down the scale of the balance. I have given
bread to the hungry and drink to him that was athirst, and have
clothed the naked with garments. I have not blasphemed. I have
not stolen. I have not made false accusation. I have not slain
any man treacherously.

The belief in immortality thus led to a desire for morality,
and religion for the first time ceased to be a matter of form
and ritual and became a matter of justice and force, a way
of life.

About the beginning of the fourteenth century before the
Christian era, there arose in Egypt the greatest religious
genius before Moses. He was an idealistic visionary who
conceived a high monotheistic belief encompassing the
whole world in its scope. To his omnipresent and omnipotent
All-father he gave the name Aton, meaning "sun" or "light."
This man was Amenhotep IV, better known to history as
Ikhnaton. He tried to establish the new faith first by persuasion and then by force. He changed his own name, Amenhotep, meaning "Amon is satisfied," to Ikhnaton, meaning
"Profitable to Aton." The whole empire was commanded by
law to accept the new religion and to give up the old polytheistic beliefs. Many of the old temples were closed, and
the priesthood was cast out to earn a living. The names of

the gods were erased from the ancient writings, and even the place of the capital was moved. Many of his people became converts. Some of the hymns of praise that he wrote are still extant, notably his great "Sun Hymn" from which we quote:

Thy dawning, O living Aton, is beautiful on the horizon. . . . O Beginning of Life, Thou art all and Thy rays encompass all. . . . Manifold are Thy works, One and Only God, whose power none other possesseth; the whole earth hast Thou created according to Thine own understanding. When Thou wast alone didst Thou create man and beast, both large and small; all that go upon their feet; all that fly upon wings; yea, all the foreign lands. . . . Thou settest all in their place, and providest all with their needs. . . . O, how goodly are Thy designs, O Lord, that there is a Nile in the sky for strangers. . . . Thou art the Life of life; through Thee men live.

But this great visionary died leaving no son to carry on. The old priesthood gained control of the new twelve-year-old successor and restored the older belief and ritual. Few relics of Ikhnaton remain, so complete was the destruction of his art, architecture, and literature by the priests of the restoration. Nevertheless, a tendency toward monotheism remained in Egypt from his time onward.

THE FERTILE CRESCENT

The people of the Fertile Crescent may be divided into three main groups. Originally nomadic, they developed into three more or less settled tribes—Babylonians, Hittites, and Assyrians. The earlier nomadic groups believed in many gods —natural objects, the gods of the watering places, and above all the tribal god who travelled with his people as they migrated from place to place. This god was an exacting one, demanding the first fruits of the flocks and herds and often human sacrifice. The earliest prayers and utterances of praise were really charms to render the evil gods powerless and to gain concessions from the good ones. There was a dawning sense of justice and right and an obligation of kindness and mercy to one's fellows, but the idea of the early Hebrews "to feed the stranger within the gates" was unknown to them.

The Babylonians in particular have left much religious literature. With them worship of the moon seems to have preceded sun worship. As time went on, a numerous pantheon was developed, with apparently no chief ruler of the gods. Among the chief deities were Assur, god of ever-reviving vegetation; Anu, king of the lower world; Bel, father of the gods and the creator; Beltis, his wife, one of the goddesses linked with the idea of the Earth Mother; Hea, determiner of destinies and lord of the harvest; Ninkigal, his wife, queen of Hades; Sin, the moon-god; Shamas, the sun-god; Vul, god of the air; Marduk, the judge; Ishtar, queen of love and beauty, goddess of marriage; Ninip, god of hunting and war; Nergal, god of war; Nebo, god of learning and knowledge (these last five later became, respectively, the Roman deities Jupiter, Venus, Saturn, Mars, and Mercury); Ashtoreth and Astarte, both Hittite goddesses of sex related to the Earth Mother. The Babylonians gave the names of the sun, moon, and five planets to the seven days of the week, and this nomenclature has survived to our own day—the names, however, changed to Roman and Teutonic forms.

Most of the Sumerian towns had a great temple tower in the center. It was nearly cubic in shape, tapering slightly toward the top. In front there were three flights of stairs, rising sometimes to a height of one hundred and fifty feet, converging on a door about half way up the tower. The upper half was a square temple open to the sky, dedicated to Vul, god of the atmosphere. The people worshipped in shrines or chapels near the base of the tower, each consisting of an open court and a sanctuary. Worship was by prayer, praise, and sacrifice. Notably absent is any allusion to a future life. The usual prayer was for a plentiful harvest and generous rainfall—a farmer's prayer. The most common sacrifice or offering was a goat and a jar of water containing palm branches, which symbolized life. The jar and the palm branch later became recognized as the "Tree of Life." The dead were usually buried in the home under the hearth—with all their belongings including bodyguards, animals, and servant for use in the gloomy dark world to which all went, whether good or bad.

Other religious symbols besides the Tree of Life are found,

notably the winged circle and the equilateral triangle. The latter, representative of the female reproductive organ, was thought to be the source of all life. The former should be compared with the Egyptian sun disk.

The Babylonian writings also leave us a record—long before Moses—of myths and legends later incorporated into the Old Testament: the creation, the deluge, the casting of Satan out of Heaven, the idea of a burning hell, the descent into Hades, and the resurrection of Ishtar. The Babylonian story of the creation is an interesting one. In the beginning was Omorka, a woman who ruled a world of chaos populated with great beasts. Bel, the creator, split Omorka in twain to make the heavens and the earth. He then split the darkness, and all animals that could not bear the light perished. The world was set in order. Bel then commanded one of his fellow gods to strike off his (Bel's) head, mix his blood with the earth, and form man therefrom. Man was thus made the partaker of divine wisdom and form. A revived Bel then made the stars, the moon, the sun, and the five planets.

Among the later Babylonians, the goddess Ishtar became the chief deity with Marduk or the fused Bel-Marduk as a second national deity. Among the lesser gods we find many trinities such as earth, sky, and sea—or the sun, moon, and Venus. Ishtar, the "Self-Waterer," was originally perhaps the wife of the spirits of wind, sun, and moon and the mistress of Tammuz, the spirit of the date palm. It was not unusual in matriarchal societies to find a goddess the chief deity. Ishtar later became a sex-dealing, life-breeding spirit, the goddess of love and marriage, probably the first of the great Earth Mother goddesses. Isis, Cybele, Beltis, Astarte, Ashtoreth, Aphrodite, and Venus are all possessed of the attributes of Ishtar.

In Babylon it was common for every woman to wait at least once in the courts of the temples of Ishtar and lie for an hour with a stranger to overcome sterility. The priests —who willingly supplied the place of the "stranger"—became rich with the price of harlotry. By the time of Hammurabi, the temples had amassed great wealth and large possessions. In many towns they were the centers of business life, trading, and banking, with interest rates as high as

20 per cent per annum. The priests had many cults, each with its own work to do—to offer sacrifice, to care for the idol, to fructify barren women, to foretell the future, and to sing the praise hymns.

The Assyrians took over most of the legends and symbols of the Babylonians, but always retained Assur, after whom they were named, as chief god. Assur was originally, like the Egyptian Osiris, a god of ever-reviving vegetation, with the Tree of Life as his symbol. Later he became associated with the sun-god, and had the additional attributes of a fierce war-god. The religion of the Assyrians carried no belief in a judgment after death, thus having little effect on their conduct and tending to make them a fierce, inhumane tribe.

The religions of the Fertile Crescent never proclaimed the rights of the humble and poor against the strong and the rich. The law was the old *lex talionis*—an eye for an eye and a tooth for a tooth. However, some of the prayers indicate a sense of sin and a fear of divine displeasure. The chief advantages of religion to these people seemed to be to avoid the displeasure of, and to obtain benefits from, the gods. The ability to foretell the future from the entrails of sacrificial animals and from the positions of the stars and planets was one of the finest gifts the gods could give. Ritual was stressed more than right living. Most of the hymns are mere repetitions of charms and spells, although some do reach a lofty spiritual pitch. Every seventh day (*Shabatum*—for Shamas, the sun-god) was regarded with special fear, a day when tabus were to be most carefully observed. This later became the Sabbath of the Jews, but with this difference, that it was a day of foreboding for the Babylonians, a day of rest and peace for the Hebrews.

THE PHALLIC CULTS

The story of primitive religion would not be complete without some brief mention of the sex religions, or phallic cults. These seem to have originated with the worship of the Earth Mother in the Fertile Crescent, who became recognized in different countries as Astarte, Isis, Cybele, Ishtar, Aphrodite, or Venus. The chief male counterparts of these deities were Baal, Osiris, Tammuz, Marduk, Adonis, and Mercury.

All followers of these phallic religions worshipped with licentious rites. About Tammuz, the spirit of the date palm, arose the myth of the tree and the serpent. The one could become the other at will, and the symbol became the phallus, or male sex organ. It is usually found together with the triangle of Ishtar, mentioned above, or with the oval symbol of Astarte or Cybele. These symbols are represented as found in the midst of the garden of paradise, emblematic of the human body. The myth in Genesis in the Old Testament concerning Eve and the Tree of Knowledge of Good and Evil may be interpreted as a veiled account of the course of sexual passion. Many survivals of the phallic cultus are extant—the Maypole, the rod of Aaron, the upright rod or cross of Osiris, the cross of the Aztecs.

One of the greatest gods of the phallic cults was the Hindu Siva. He, with Vishnu and Brahma, made up the main triad of these peoples. He was worshipped as the god of destruction and reproduction. Even today, there are about three million followers of Siva in India, known as the *Lingayat*. The name is derived from the fact that they wear as an ornament about the neck the phallic symbol, or linga —an upright cylindrical block resting on an oval stone with a hole in the center. Siva is usually represented as seated in a thinking posture, and as having four hands, three eyes, and a necklace of skulls.

The worshippers of Vishnu and Siva worshipped with licentious rites, but they permitted no bloodshed. Widows were permitted to remarry—an unusual custom among early peoples. Cremation and child marriage were forbidden. In the present Lingayat there are three castes: the pure, made up of priests and chief traders; the affiliated, consisting of those initiated into the eightfold sacrament; and lower groups, not recognized the equals of the first two.

The phallic religions are important for their contribution to the cultural side of civilization. Out of their rites in the times of the Greeks arose the Dionysiac festival with its *tragos*, or goat song. This was the origin and the forerunner of that great branch of literature and entertainment known as the drama.

Chapter III

Mythology

MYTHOLOGY includes all or any of the following: explanations of the creation of the world and man, explanations of natural phenomena such as sunrise and seasonal changes, stories of supernatural beings and their adventures, sacred tales and stories, explanation of gods and rituals. We find the most highly developed and complete mythologies among the Greeks, the Romans (who simply adapted the Greek pantheon to their own times and needs), and the northern Teutons, or Norsemen.

THE OLYMPIC GODS

The early Greek thought of spirits or gods in all natural objects. Each had a particular limited sphere of influence. One could ordinarily gain favor or avoid displeasure by making a simple gift. This later became a blood sacrifice or the smoke of a burnt offering. The religion was essentially an outdoor one, because of the mild Mediterranean climate, and no temples are found in the early period. Later, about the time of Pericles in Athens, temple building became popular, but even then the temples were memorials and offerings of praise or thanksgiving rather than places of worship. The gods were like human beings in form and attributes, possessed of the same frailties and weaknesses of character. This resulted in little moral significance being attached to religion. The difference between gods and men lay in the greater strength and beauty and in the immortality of the former. Burial customs were varied, some groups using cremation, others preservation and burial of the corpse. At death it was believed that most men passed to a gloomy, dark, dreary spirit world, whereas a few heroes passed to the Elysian Fields far to the west. Even this more desirable place was not one to be sought by the lusty Greeks. One of their great heroes is reported to have said that it would be better to be least in the kingdom of man than to rule in the kingdom of the dead.

For many centuries in Greece the Olympic pantheon held sway. The home of the gods was Mount Olympus, and hence the name. Zeus was the greatest of the gods, the father of mankind, the god of weather, rain, and thunder, with the oak tree sacred to him. His mother was Rhea, the Earth Mother or fertility goddess of the Minoans of the Aegean area. Pluto, or Hades, was one of his two brothers and ruled the netherworld. The other brother was Poseidon, usually represented with a trident, who ruled the sea and had power to cause storms and earthquakes. Hera, the protectress of marriage, was the wife of Zeus. Together with Artemis, the divine huntress, and Hermes, the god of commerce, patron of intercourse and messenger of the gods, she was one of the three chief moon-spirits. Apollo became the favorite son of Zeus. He was born in the island of Delos, the twin brother of Artemis. He is usually represented as tall, handsome, and beardless, sometimes carrying a bow with golden arrows, sometimes a lyre. He was the god of disease, pestilence, and healing, of archery and music, the patron who shielded the flocks of the shepherd and the crops of the farmer, later a sun-god. He had extensive power to foretell the future as ordained by Zeus and hence became a great favorite in the later mystery religions. Aesculapius, his son, was god of medicine.

Athena, the daughter of Zeus, according to a very old legend, was conceived in the brain of her father and leaped forth fully armed. She was a warrior goddess who ruled the air and who protected the Greek cities in war and peace. She was chosen the patroness of Athens because she brought the gift of the olive tree to the Athenians. Highly regarded, she was the wisest and loveliest of the protecting forces. In the time of Pericles, the Athenians made a great wooden, gold-plated statue of her on the Acropolis—so tall that the sun glinting on the tip of her golden spear could be seen forty miles out to sea. This statue was one of the Seven Wonders of the Ancient World, but was destroyed by barbarians for the sake of the gold it contained.

Aphrodite, perhaps also a daughter of Zeus, compares to the sexual goddesses of the East—Cybele, Ishtar, and Astarte. Her husband was Hephaestus, god of fire, but she is noted for her amours with several others. By one of her lovers she became the mother of Eros. Her worship was often marked by sexual excesses. Sacred to her were the goat, the deer, the dove, the rose, and the myrtle. Eros, or Cupid, her son, was the god of sensual love. He is always pictured as armed with a bow and two kinds of arrows, one of which engendered love, and the other hate. Adonis was the best loved of the youths favored by Aphrodite. After his death she so mourned for him that Zeus permitted him to spend alternately six months among the living and six months with the dead. Thus, he became worshipped as an ever-reviving spirit of vegetation.

A pretty myth grew up about Psyche, the allegorical human soul which eventually found complete happiness through a purification of sorrow and trouble. She was a maiden so beautiful that Aphrodite became jealous of her and sent Eros to make her fall in love with the meanest of men. When Eros spied her, he himself fell in love with her, and then left her. Psyche sought him, weeping bitterly, until she at last was united with him and became immortal.

There were many other divinities in the Greek pantheon. To mention only a few of the lesser ones, we have Demeter, goddess of the harvest; Hestia, goddess of the hearth; Orpheus, god of music; and Dionysus, god of the vineyards. From the festivals held for Dionysus developed the use of drama as a means of entertainment as well as worship.

There was neither great fear nor great love of these superhuman gods. Men possessing outstanding knowledge slowly developed a priesthood. Literature and drama, encouraged by the government, became associated with the festivals, especially the Dionysiac wine feasts. To gain salvation, the Greeks developed a number of mystery cults. Usually these called for an initiation, essentially sensual in nature, involving gluttony, drunkenness, and emotionality, through which immortality could be gained. The Eleusinian mystery, much colder and more formal, dates back probably to 1000 B.C. About the sixth century B.C. came the Orphic cult and still later the Egyptian Osiris cult and the Phrygian

Attis cult, all with a sensual basis. Some of these still flourished even after Christianity came—and the Greeks would have made a mystery cult of it, too, had they been able.

In Rome the earliest religion was centered in the family. The Romans worshipped Genius, or virility, in man, and in woman, Juno, the power to conceive. The other deities were primarily of the individual family, though similar gods were called by the same name throughout Rome. The four chief family gods were Janus, the two-faced guardian of the household, usually represented on the door of the home with one face inward and the other outward; Lar, god of the farm and the harvest; Penate, guardian of the storeroom; and Vesta, guardian of the hearth. The father was priest, judge, and king in his own family.

Later the Romans developed a state religion, taking over the family gods and most of the older Greek gods, but giving the latter new Latin names. Jupiter—king of the gods, a sky-god, god of rain, thunder, and lightning, god of hospitality, truth, and justice, god of the growth of fruits, later a war-god—became chief god of the Romans and compares to the Greek Zeus. Mars was one of the few original Roman gods—the god of war. Venus, the Greek Aphrodite, queen of love, was originally a goddess of gardens. She became a chief deity as the wife of Mars and the mother of Aeneas, the founder of the race. Neptune, god of the sea, was the Roman Poseidon. Juno (Hera), a sky goddess, was protectress of women, birth, and marriage. Vesta, guardian of hearth and household, had a perpetual fire tended by virgin priestesses in her temples. Ceres (Demeter) was goddess of the harvest—from her name comes our common word "cereal." Mercury (Hermes) was the winged messenger of the gods, the patron of intercourse and merchandising (this latter word deriving from his name).

The Roman gods were never as immoral or sensual as were the Greek Olympic gods, but neither were they as puritanical as the Hebrew Yahveh. The Roman religion was clean, but cold. The Roman lacked the imagination of the Greek, and this explains his coldly calculating attitude towards his gods. The Delphic oracles were recorded in the Sibylline Books and regarded as a revelation of the future. The Roman priest could also foretell the future from the entrails of animals. The Roman looked upon religion as the fulfillment of a contract and drove hard, sometimes sharp, bargains with his gods.

About 200 B.C. mystery cults began to appear just as they had earlier in Greece. Most notable was the Cybele cult, centered on Vatican hill, its festivals marked by blood guzzling, self-mutilation, and dancing. Associated with the Cybele cult was that of her lover, Attis (the older Tammuz, Osiris, Dionysus, or Orpheus under a new name). He was a god of ever-reviving vegetation. Born of a virgin, he died and was reborn annually. The festival began as a day of blood on Black Friday and culminated after three days in a day of rejoicing over the resurrection. Note the extremely close parallel between the Attis festival and the festival of Easter adopted by the Christian Church about three cen-turies later—the Vatican center, the three-day period from Friday to Sunday, the idea of a death and a resurrection.

Two other Roman festivals should be noted, one of them because it looked backward to the Greeks and earlier peo-ples, and the other because it pointed forward to the most popular Christian festival. In the Lupercalia men smeared with blood and goat's milk and clad in goatskins danced through the streets of Rome striking the women with bits of skin to make them fertile. This was a direct descendant of the Greek Dionysiac festival, which in turn can be traced back to the Ishtar courts custom for the same purpose. The Ro-man Saturnalia, held on December 25th, was one of the bright-est of all the festivals of early times. It was taken over prac-tically intact by the later peoples as the Christian festival of Christmas. Even the date was taken over and accepted as the one on which to celebrate the birthday of Jesus Christ, a date which is unknown but historically must have been at an altogether different time of year. During the Saturnalia we find only good things—dancing, feasting, merrymaking, forgiveness of debts, candle-lighting ceremonies, and gift giving. More will be said later of the debt which Chris-tianity and Christian customs owe to earlier, more ancient religious forms.

NORSE MYTHOLOGY

The early Teutons and Norse peoples are found to be both animistic and anthropomorphic. They seem to have neither a carefully organized system of religion nor a regular priesthood. They thought all things, animate and inanimate, possessed spirits like their own. They leave a conglomeration of tales of gods and goddesses of the sun, the sky, the earth, the moon, and the afterworld. Dreams were thought to be a forecast of events to come when properly interpreted. Wizardry and magic made up a part of the beliefs. The dead were sometimes worshipped.

They thought the world to be a vast plain, with man living near its edge. All natural phenomena could be explained through their mythology as the outcome of actions of gods and men. Their temples were meeting places, treasuries, and storehouses. Their rituals often contained elements of both animal and human sacrifice. Once or twice a year, depending on the wealth of the community, there was a great cattle sacrifice. After the populace had been sprinkled with the blood and auguries had been duly taken, the flesh of the sacrifice was used for a great feast. There is an absence of the sensuality and sexuality noted in the religions already studied, and some historians and scholars attribute this to the colder, less enervating, and more vigorous climate.

The black magic of the witch or wizard, established by mania, hysteria, hypnotism, poison, jugglery, etc., was dreaded and abhorred, sometimes punished. On the other hand, the white magic of the seers, dream readers, and weather prophets was honored and reverenced.

Good manners and morals were taught in song and story. The virtues of these people were courage, manliness, upright living, cleanliness, sincerity, generosity, silence, and reverence. Coupled with this fine teaching we find false ideas of honor and pride, a weakness expressed in superstitious fears and deceit, harshness, and cruelty toward all nonmembers of the tribe or clan.

At least three ideas of future life were extant among these people. The heroes were thought to undergo transmigration, spending eternity in Valhalla. Another common belief was that the soul remained in the grave. The third was that the soul fell into the great abyss of the goddess Hela. If it was possessed of the virtues mentioned above, it might win past the demons to a happier sphere. The evildoer, if not punished in this life, would gain fit recompense hereafter.

The supernatural beings fell into two groups—the giants and the gods. The former were evil, almost always at variance with gods and men. From the body of the giant Ymir, Odin, the All-father, had created the heavens and the earth. Loki was another giant, beautiful, cunning, and malignant, the god of fire as a destructive agent. His son was Fenris, the wolf; and his daughter was Hel or Hela, queen of the underworld and the dead. She was completely evil, with "care her bed, hunger her dish, and starvation her knife."

The gods lived in Asgard, much as the Greek gods lived on Olympus. Chief of the gods was Odin, the patron of culture, god of wisdom, poetry, magic, and prophecy. He had only one eye, because with the other he had purchased wisdom from Mimir, guardian of the fountain of wisdom, that he might spread it among men. As the Celtic god, Wodan (Madness), he became a god of courage and war, and gave his name to the middle day of the week. Thor, god of thunder, wind, rain, clear weather, and good crops, was the eldest son of Odin. His mother was Jord, the earth, and his wife was Sif, the cornfield. He was the implacable foe of the giants, and survives today as the source of the name Thursday. Fricco, god of generation, gave peace and pleasure.

Balder, the sun-god, husband of Nanna, the moon-goddess, and a younger son of Odin, was best-loved of the gods. He was an ever-reviving god like Attis, Tammuz, and Osiris. Early in life he dreamed of evil, and so his mother went over the world making all things promise never to harm Balder—but she missed the lowly mistletoe. Loki, by a ruse, discovered this fact, and made a dart of a mistletoe branch. One day in sport the gods were all throwing their weapons and missiles at Balder to prove his invulnerability. Loki aided the blind god Hoder to throw the dart which he had made, and killed Balder. The gods sent to Hela's realm to beg him back, but she would give him up only on condition that the whole world should weep. Loki, disguised as an old hag, refused to weep, and thus Balder could not be freed.

Deserving of mention is Valhalla, Odin's hall of heroes

in Asgard, the Norse heroes' heaven. The Valkyries, warrior maidens of Odin, selected those brave enough to be brought to Valhalla. These maidens lived in Valhalla also, another of their duties being to pass mead at the feasts. The hall itself was described as being thatched with the shields of the heroes, hung with their armor and mail, and lit with swords as tapers. Here battles were fought by day and feasting was carried on at night. From each of its five hundred and forty doors it was said that eight hundred warriors would issue for the last great fight with the giants when the end of the world would come.

CONCLUSION

Mythology is sometimes referred to as a "natural" religion. Notice how, in all three of the above groups, the outstanding factors in man's life—earth, moon, harvest, love, marriage, sun, war, death, knowledge, etc.—are each represented by a god or goddess. These were the things common, or "natural," to all men. It is a fascinating pastime to trace parallels in the beliefs of peoples who had no outside contact with each other. These parallels seem to indicate that certain things are basic, one might almost say innate, in the make-up of humankind.

Chapter IV

Ancient Religious Beliefs in the Americas

In the Western Hemisphere, we find primitive religions still flourishing in the sixteenth century, when the white man came. This fact enables us to gain a clearer account of these beliefs than is available of the more truly ancient religions.

RELIGION OF THE AZTECS

Most highly developed were the Aztecs of Mexico, with a polytheism and a highly organized and numerous priestly hierarchy.

By the time the whites came to America, the Aztec religion was largely controlled by this priesthood. Careful analysis of their customs seem to reveal two sources of their beliefs—an early mild form overlaid with a veneer of ferocity at some later date. There is evidence that originally they were a monotheistic group, and the Supreme Being of this early faith remains in the later polytheistic pantheon as an omniscient and omnipresent deity. By the sixteenth century, there were many gods—thirteen principal deities and approximately two hundred lesser gods. Their mythology tells of four distinct eras or periods in the past, at the end of each of which man was completely destroyed and later reestablished on a new and higher plane.

Temples were numerous, one city of three hundred thousand population reporting over six hundred of them. They provided homes for the numerous priests when the latter were in attendance on the deity. The temple was a solid mound, built like a storied pyramid. Stairs went up the outside—sometimes straight up the west side, but usually at a fixed angle up each flight with a gallery all the way around the temple to the next flight. This latter arrangement necessitated several circuits of the temple before the summit was reached. Hence all the community could see a procession, even from a great distance. At the top was a tall sanctuary, with a sacrificial altar in front of it between two fire altars. On the latter, the priest maintained perpetual fires (compare the Roman Vesta). So numerous were the temples that at night some cities were well lighted by these altar fires. All religious services were public, most of the festivals being light and cheerful, but with an occasional dismal one. Each temple was supported by gifts and donations as well as by the produce from the lands it owned. All surplus was used for charity, thus preventing the priesthood from becoming too rich.

The chief deity became the sun, and as further evidence of an early mild religion there is no record of general human sacrifice to this god, Tezcatlepoca. To him there was a single annual sacrifice of one victim, chosen a year in advance. This particular sacrifice dates from the fourteenth century. During the year of preparation, the victim was accorded the highest honors, as to one representative of the highest deity. He led an easy, luxurious life and was attended by four beautiful maidens appointed to gratify his every whim. On the day appointed for completion of the sacrificial rite, six priests led a procession of the whole community through the streets and up to the altar of the temple. In a terrible awe-inspiring finale, five of the priests garbed in black stretched the victim out on the slightly convex sacrificial altar—one at each extremity and one at the head. The high priest, in a long crimson robe, poised aloft the sacrificial knife, then with a single surgeon's stroke lay open the naked breast of the offering, tore out the still-beating heart and showed it to the sun and the populace before casting it at the feet of the idol. The body of the sacrificial victim was then prepared as a feast for all, regarded as a sacrament similar to the Christian Eucharist and not degrading to the partakers of it. This ritual cannibalism in their religion may indicate an earlier general cannibalism among these people, because it is unlikely that a sacrifice unpalatable to man would be offered to the god.

Most feared and most placated of the deities was the war-god Huitzilopotchli, the patron god of the state. He is represented in the temples with a fantastic image. His temples are always huge and richly adorned, with a prominent sacrificial stone, for he demanded human sacrifice in large numbers. Most of his victims were prisoners of war. We find that the Aztecs had a treaty with a friendly and peaceful neighboring tribe to meet annually in a certain place for a battle with the sole purpose of obtaining captives on both sides for sacrificial purposes.

Another important and greatly loved deity was the god of the air, Quetzalcoatl, the regenerative god of the Aztecs. He did not require human sacrifice, encouraged asceticism, and had a large following among the better classes. He is described as beautiful, tall, white-skinned, and black-haired. His description tallies with that of Osiris, Attis, Tammuz, or Apollo. While with man on earth he had taught the arts of government, of the use of metals, and of agriculture. His was the Golden Age of the Aztecs. The belief that he was to return made the way easier for the white-skinned, black-haired Spanish conquistador Cortez in the early sixteenth century when he came to America.

Xiuhtecutli, god of fire, was another principal deity. With him we find an example of early symbolism in sacrifice. A dough image of the god was raised on a cross, climbed for by the young men, and thrown down among the multitude that all might partake of the sacrament. The goddess of water, Cioacoatl, was honored in the festival of infant baptism. Her husband was Tlaloc, the rain-god. There was also a goddess of love who was worshipped with some sensuality, but in general, celibacy was highly regarded among Aztec men.

The numerous priesthood was classified into a regular hierarchy, each class with its own special duties, such as performance of sacrificial rites, keeping records, tending the altar fires, caring for education of the young. At the head were two high priests, equal in rank, and subordinate only to the king in power. The lesser priests lived in the temples under strict conventual rule during their periods of service to the deity. They had a very strict rule of penance, vigils, ablutions, fasting, and prayer—the prayers repeated three times daily and once during the night. When not in attendance on the god, these priests were permitted to live "out" with their own wives and families if they so desired, but many of them were celibate. The sense of duty was developed to the point of fanaticism, sometimes of hysteria. They abhorred sensual indulgences, and had a highly developed spirit of self-sacrifice leading to severe asceticism. Many saints are found among them.

Education was in the hands of one group of the priests. The girls were instructed by priestesses in the household arts, the boys by the priests who had care of temples and of the sacred altar fires, in astronomy, in principles of government, and in the ancient lore and hieroglyphics of the Aztecs. Moral discipline was most strict, and the highest moral ideas were inculcated. They were taught to seek peace, to bear injuries meekly, to be charitable, to rely on God's love and mercy. At the age of entering into the world, these students graduated with great ceremony from the convent, many of them being recommended to high political posts.

The priests also had charge of all sacrifices. Among peoples with a limited priesthood, human sacrifice early becomes symbolical; but where the priesthood is extensive, the ritual seems to be retained and extended. We have already seen a symbolical crucifixion practiced by the Aztecs. The Christians maintain the idea of a single human sacrifice symbolically through the sacrament—and there is good evidence that the Eucharist was originally a baked-dough image of the Saviour. Some of the human sacrifices of the Aztecs have been already mentioned. Occasionally, but rarely, there was torture first, perhaps to test the fitness of the victim. The goddesses required sacrifices of female victims. Infant sacrifice was demanded by the rain-god, Tlaloc, in time of drought. For this rite sucking infants were extorted from superstitious parents or purchased from poor ones.

Confession of sins and absolution were practiced, and these rites also were under the direction of the priesthood. Absolution and penance took the place of legal punishment. An offense confessed and atoned for and later repeated was considered inexpiable. Therefore, each man usually confessed only once, toward the end of his lifetime. At death a corpse was dressed in the costume of its special deity, covered with bits of paper to act as charms in warding off evil (compare here the Egyptian Book of the Dead), and burned. If the man were rich, numerous slaves would be sacrificed to accompany him. His ashes were collected and preserved in a vase and kept reverently in the home. In the future life the wicked expiated their sins in a place of everlasting darkness, and the good were rewarded. A few who died of certain specified diseases (for no other apparent reason) spent the afterlife in a world of lazy contentment and peace. Warriors who fell in battle and those who died in sacrifice passed immediately to a home in the sun, a place of pleasure and song. Later they went to paradise, a land of flowers and singing birds, where they were rewarded with all the luxuries and comforts a man could desire.

There are many parallels with Christian teachings. In their ritual of naming children we find a very similar act to Christian baptism. The lips and breast of the infant were sprinkled with water, and "God" was implored to take away the sin given the child before the foundation of the world. Some of these quotations from their writings and prayers might be compared to Christian teaching:

1. Clothe the naked and feed the hungry, whatever privation it may cost thee.
2. Cherish the sick for they are the image of God.
3. He who looks too curiously upon a woman commits adultery with his eyes.
4. Impart to us, out of thy great mercy, thy gifts which we are not worthy to receive through our own merit.

RELIGION OF THE INCAS

Another great religious society or nation in America was the Incas of Peru, so-called from the family name of their rulers. Probably in earliest times they had been nature-worshipping cannibals with war a chief pastime, but by the time the European explorers came in the sixteenth century they had developed a very high civilization with an architecture at least the equal of anything in the Old World.

According to their legends the Great Sun Father sent two of his children, Manco Capac and Mama Oello Huaco, to teach the arts of civilization to his people. He gave them a great golden wedge and told them that they were to travel until it sank without effort into the ground, and at that point they were to set up the center of the nation. The wedge disappeared in the valley of Cuzco (meaning "navel") near Lake Titicaca in the central part of Peru. The Temple of the Sun in Cuzco was the most magnificent, the richest, and the most elaborate building in the Americas, and rivalled in greatness anything of the ancient or medieval world.

The two children of the Sun married, and their descendants were the Incas, who ruled by divine right because of their divine origin. To preserve and maintain the divinity of the line, every Inca married his eldest sister and the descendants of this marriage succeeded to the throne. The lawful queen became known as the Coya, and all her children had a specially privileged rank. Cranial measurement of Inca remains indicates that inbreeding in this family produced men of superior mental caliber. Unlimited polygamy was permitted the Inca, although the Coya was always lawful queen. The progeny of the Inca's unions seems to have been numerous —in some cases upwards of three hundred children, according to certain accounts. All these children were called Incas and had noble rank—many of them secured the highest positions in church, government, army, and society. The Inca himself was a benevolent despot, holding the position of chief priest, judge, and army leader.

The successor to the throne was especially instructed in military affairs. At the age of sixteen, or puberty, he was put through initiatory rites combining mental, spiritual, and physical instruction and tests. At the death of the Inca, special burial rites were practiced. The entrails were removed and buried, and on his tomb many servants and concubines were immolated. Suttee was widely practiced, good widows, with the exception of the Coya, being buried alive. The body of the Inca was embalmed and placed in a seated position on the right of the aisle in the Temple of the Sun at Cuzco. The body of the Coya was likewise embalmed and placed facing that of the Inca on the left of the aisle. Thus did these people preserve their dead rulers for future generations to see.

The two leading deities were Pachacamac and Viracocha, heat and moisture, both of them creators. One theory is that this may indicate the fusion of two tribes, another that they originally symbolized the female and male elements respectively in generation. The thunder and lightning were worshipped as ministers to the sun-god, and the rainbow as his symbol. The moon, the stars, and Venus were worshipped as separate deities. Perpetual fires were maintained on the altars and renewed annually by a special ritual in which new fire was made with concave mirrors. This perpetual fire ritual is one of the oldest religious rites. The Aztecs regenerated their altar fires by friction in a great festival every fifty-second year. The Romans maintained a perpetual fire in the temples of Vesta. The Christian custom of lighted candles before the images of the saints or on the altars in some churches may have its origin in earlier pagan rites.

There is evidence that some of the Incas were freethinkers. They noted that even the great Sun was regulated in his course, and therefore must not be the supreme authority. From this fact sprang a belief in a supernatural god superior to the sun.

Rites of infant baptism and confession of sins were practiced. Infant sacrifice was replaced by a ritual in which blood was drawn but the life spared (a practice which should be compared to that of circumcision of males). There is a trace in the story of Abraham and Isaac in the Old Testament of the Inca custom of offering a son for the sins of the father. The Incas had a Holy Communion ritual, using a sacred bread called the sancu sprinkled with the blood of a sacrificial sheep. The following is a quotation from the ritual:

Take heed how you eat this sancu; for he who eats it in sin, and with a double will and heart, is seen by our Father, the Sun, who will punish him with grievous trouble. But he who with a single heart partakes of it, to him the Sun and the Thunderer will show favor, and will grant children and happy years, and abundance of all he requires.

The people under the Inca regime were oppressed with severe laws and tyrannous taxes. From the taxes the nobles and clergy, mostly of the Inca family, were exempt. As one good result of the small, limited priesthood, human sacrifices were few. Material well-being of a very high degree was attained. The cities had clean, well-lighted streets, and the Incas surpassed all Europeans except the Romans in the arts of road building, law administration, architecture, and agriculture. In general, we may say that they reached the highest civilization of primitive people in the Western Hemisphere and were more advanced than any of the early peoples of Europe, Africa, or the Near East.

Chapter V

Judaism—The Faith of the Hebrews

THE early Hebrews were similar in every respect to their neighbors. They believed in the same supernatural beings, in holy trees, holy wells, holy stones, and other similar fetishes. It is quite probable that the Ark carried through the desert to the Promised Land contained a stone of meteoric origin. Since the Hebrews had no conception of the universe it was impossible for them to formulate the idea of supreme infinite god. Yahveh, or Jahveh, later Jehovah, like all primitive gods, was a spiritual being, rather more easily roused to wrath than most of the early deities. He was not the loving Father pictured by David in later times, but a jealous god —a demanding deity who forced his followers to give up all other gods and even to forsake worship of ancestors. In the early period, he was neither omnipresent, omniscient, nor omnipotent.

Each village had its place of worship, and idols have been found from time to time. Yahveh revealed himself and the future in dreams and revelations. Any father could make sacrifice, usually a burnt offering of first fruits of crops and herds but sometimes a human sacrifice. The early priests were caretakers of the holy places and sanctuaries. As in all early religions, sacrifice was a gift either to beg the deity to show favor or to express gratitude for favors already bestowed. As in all animistic religions, there were tabus of abstinence, cleanliness, clean and unclean foods, curses and blessings. The blessing of the father was especially esteemed, and belonged in the ordinary course of events to the eldest son. Witness the tale of Jacob and Esau, with the extreme lengths to which Jacob went to get the blessing which should have belonged to the elder brother. Festivals included the usual spring and harvest festivals of an agricultural or pastoral people, and lunar feasts.

In the early period the moral grandeur of Yahveh was revealed only by a few prophets. To them there was no difference between physical and moral evil, no duty to any save their own countrymen. Sin against Yahveh and crime against the tribe were one and the same. It was equally bad deliberately to break a law or inadvertently to do so— ignorance of the law was no excuse. In the earliest period one man's sin might bring retribution on the whole tribe; but later, punishment was meted out to the individual only.

Abraham is the first truly historical figure among them. He left Ur in Chaldea with the Hebrew tribe about 2000 B.C. After a period of nomadic peregrination in the Arabian desert and Egypt, they at last settled in the latter country, where they were later enslaved. About 1200 B.C. their greatest historian, Moses, a Hebrew foundling raised in Pharaoh's palace, led his people out of the Egyptian bondage.

Legend has it that Yahveh opened a path through the Red Sea for Moses and his followers. Modern science reveals that an earthquake possibly could be the explanation of the miracle. Be that as it may, after a period of travail and further nomadic wanderings, the Hebrews finally settled in Palestine, the Promised Land of the Old Testament. During this time under the direction of Moses, the first five books of what later was to become the Old Testament were written —the tales of the Creation, the Garden of Eden, the Fall of Adam, Noah and his Ark, and the ancient Mosaic Law of the Ten Commandments.

Shortly after the settlement in Palestine, about 1000 B.C., the Hebrews organized themselves into the Kingdom of Israel. Three kings ruled successively over this kingdom: Saul, the war lord; David, who left much of that section of the Old Testament known as the "Psalms"; and Solomon, the king of wisdom, best known for the collection of wise saws known as the "Proverbs," and for the first building of the temple at Jerusalem. After the reign of Solomon, the kingdom broke in twain, Israel with its capital at Samaria, and Judah with its capital at Jerusalem.

This change in the history of the people brought a corresponding change in religion. Israel was a wealthy nation of town dwellers who accepted the customs and gods (or baals) of the neighboring Canaanites. Judah was a poor nation of farmers and shepherds who clung to the ancient Yahveh. Baal thus became the god of the rich, Yahveh the support of the poor. The Prophets belonged to this period and supported their god vociferously, sometimes violently. Elijah proclaimed war between Yahveh and Baal, calling down punishment on those who followed the easy ways of town life. The Israelite royal family and the Canaanite priests were slain, but with no lasting religious revival—Yahveh remained a war-god belonging exclusively to the Hebrews.

Also to this period belongs a body of writing about "the good old days," a flowery account of the times of Isaac and Jacob when the land flowed with milk and honey. The writers, being acquainted with the works of Egyptian social reformers and philosophers of an earlier day, incorporated their philosophies and proverbs in defense of the poor and helpless into their own writings.

With the prophets Amos, Hosea, and the Second Isaiah, circa 750 B.C., religion changed from a ceremonial ritual to a way of life. Fear of God became love of God, and religion became a social force. Amos interpreted God as just, as a universal Father rather than a tribal war-god, as a god who rebuked the oppressors and the selfish. Amos was the first great social reformer in Asia, denouncing the high life and corrupt practices of the northern towns, condemning the hard-hearted selfishness of Hebrew to Hebrew, and pointing out the way to altruistic living, brotherly love, and a higher form of religion. No doubt much of the old Egyptian teachings of kindness and justice to the weak and humble was incorporated. Amos also made another great historical stride forward—he wrote down his teachings to ensure their preservation.

When the Assyrians destroyed Israel in 722 B.C., Yahveh became entrenched against Assur. Isaiah was the prophet of this period, and he began to proclaim Yahveh as a universal god, omnipotent and omnipresent. He it was who foretold the destruction of the Assyrian host under Sennacherib because the latter opposed Yahveh.

Judah was invaded and the people were taken into the "Babylonian Captivity" by Nebuchadnezzar in 586 B.C. Some fled to Egypt with Jeremiah, others retained their belief in Yahveh in Babylonia. To them also he became the sole

Creator, the All-father of the universe, who disciplined his followers by suffering.

The Captivity added much to their philosophy and theology. The Talmud, partly written during the Captivity, shows many parallels with the Babylonian law. From the Babylonians, the Hebrews absorbed the *lex talionis*—the law of an eye for an eye, a tooth for a tooth. Note also the close parallel between the Sun Hymn of Ikhnaton and Psalm 104.

The Sun Hymn:

> How manifold are Thy Works!
> They are hidden before men
> O Sole God, beside whom there is no other.
> Thou didst create the earth according to Thy will.

The Psalm:

> O Lord! How manifold are Thy works!
> In wisdom hast Thou made them all—
> The earth is full of Thy riches.

After the Persians had conquered the Fertile Crescent, Cyrus restored the Hebrews to Palestine. At Jerusalem the temple was rebuilt. All the ancient writings, the books of the Prophets, and the Psalms were collected. The Talmud —a compendium of detailed laws for guidance of civil, domestic, and social life—was completed. The new restored state was really a religious organization, or church, with the priest at the head. The Law, the Psalms, and the Prophets remained as separate holy books until the time of Christ when they were organized into the Hebrew Bible, or as it is better known to us, the Christian Old Testament. The Hebrew state church was overrun by Alexander the Great, and later by the Romans, who ruled during the time of Christ. About 135 A.D. came the final Diaspora, or dispersal, and since that time the Jews have been a religious group without a country, interspersed among many varying national groups.

Judaism is a reasonable and moderate belief, countenancing no excess or extravagance. The central truth of its teaching is that the final aim of religion, the *summum bonum*, is morality. In this it differs from the more extensive religions —Hinduism, which makes ritual perfection the end, and

Christianity, which makes faith more important than good works. To the Jews, right conduct in everyday life is more important than right belief. According to the Talmud, every good man is assured of Heaven, the heathen who observes the moral law being the equal of the high priest. Judaism is a truly catholic belief: "Thou shalt love thy neighbor as thyself." The Hebrew is bound to visit the sick, to relieve the poor, to bury the dead, without regard to religion. Loans are preferable to charitable gifts among them because they do not detract from self-respect. Judaism is free from sentimentalism. Self-imposed suffering, idleness, and asceticism are frowned upon. Manliness is a dominant note. Female worth is highly regarded. Humane treatment of lower animals is demanded. The milder virtues of meekness and humility are commended. An eleventh-century Hebrew writer sums up the teaching thus: "Speak the truth; be modest; live on the coarsest fare rather than be dependent on others. Shun evil companions, be not like flies that swarm in foul places. Rejoice not when thine enemy falls; be not both witness and judge; avoid anger, the heritage of fools." The following passage from the Talmud should be compared with Aristotle's theory of the Golden Mean: "The Law may be likened to two roads, one of fire, the other of snow. To follow the one is to perish by fire; to follow the other is to die of the cold. The middle path alone is safe."

Chapter VI

Zoroastrianism

OUT of Persia was to come one of the highest and most philosophical conceptions of deity before the time of Christ. The Persians started with the same animistic and primitive tendencies as other peoples of their time, but about 660 B.C. a man-child was born in Media, a neighboring state, who was to bring forth a highly enlightened religion. This was Zarathustra or Zoroaster. He was, according to legend, a wonder-child, born of an immaculate conception, who attained salvation suddenly and preached a religion well suited to the needs of the people on the Iranian plateaus with their tough struggle for survival.

He taught that life was a struggle between the forces of Good and of Evil, the world serving as the battleground on which there could be no neutrals. Each man must choose the side on which he would stand, and in making the choice he must bear in mind the judgment hereafter. There was no room for sentimentality. The choice was hard, and the work was hard as life itself. No mercy could be shown the enemy, whether man, beast, or weed. Good works, including irrigation, sowing and reaping, rearing of domestic animals, all were admired and encouraged.

The spirit of good was Ahura Mazda, Lord of Wisdom, with his helper, Mithras, Light. The evil spirit was Aingra Mainyu, or Ahriman, the Lie Demon. The two great spirits had come together for the Creation, Ahura Mazda creating everything except moral and physical evil, which things were established by Ahriman. Ahura Mazda had six leading attributes: the good mind, or love; the righteous order, or plan of grace; Khshathra, or divine noble government; Armaiti, or holy character, or piety; Haurvatat, or health of mind and body; and Immortality, or life perpetuated in a heaven of

36

good thoughts, words, and deeds. Ahura Mazda was supported by Mithras, Light, and hence the veneration of fire as a symbol and the retention of the fire priests. Ahriman gained assistance from the old idols and gods.

Man, as has been said, could not be neutral in the great struggle. The test was the uprightness of his life and the assistance his conduct gave against evil. The emphasis was upon his works. Thus did Zoroaster give for the first time in history an answer to the question, "Why is life?" He said, "To fight for the right." The Zoroastrian believed in a paradise and a hell. The pious after death went to an immortality of holiness in thought, word, and deed—not to a sensual heaven as found in many religions. The impious fell from the Judge's Bridge into an eternal hell of evil thoughts, words, and deeds, and of physical torment.

In the days of the end-time all the dead would be restored by a Saviour born of the seed of Zoroaster and a virgin who was to conceive in a lake impregnated with his semen. The good and the evil would join in a great battle known as "The Affair," from which, after a period of doubt and darkness, Ahura Mazda would emerge victorious. Then all the hills and mountains would melt and pour over the earth in a great flood. Every wicked thing would perish as though scalded, but the righteous would wade through with laughter, as though through a bath of warm milk. The earth would then be a paradise with no mountains or deserts, no savages or wild beasts, where the just would live on forever with joy and gladness in their hearts.

Zoroastrianism was too noble and too advanced for its time. Zoroaster was spurned by his own people, the Medes, and took his beliefs to the Persians. Here he was not in his lifetime accepted either, but by 500 B.C. Zoroastrianism had become the leading faith of the Persians. His hymns and fragments of his teachings and sayings were gathered into a book which became the Persian Bible, the Avesta, or Zend-Avesta. Zoroastrianism led to government in Persia more just than anywhere else in the ancient East. The emperors were given a sense of obligation, as witness this quotation from Darius, "Ahura Mazda brought me help because I was not wicked, nor was I a liar, nor was I a tyrant. I have ruled according to righteousness."

Zoroastrianism degenerated in the hands of later genera-tions to a theological ritual. Mithras grew in importance, and cults devoted to him spread as far west as Rome, some relics of his rites being found even on the Seine. Elaborate purifica-tion rites became the vogue—most notable being a purifica-tion by a bath from head to foot in cow urine. The dead were thought unholy, and tabu was placed on the touching of a corpse. To this day, where Zoroastrianism survives, bodies cannot be burned or buried, but are left exposed to scavenging vultures.

The most numerous sect of Zoroastrians existent today is the Parsees in India, numbering about eighty-four thousand. They are descendants of Persian refugees who in the seventh and eighth centuries were permitted to settle in India on condition of laying down their arms, refraining from killing the sacred cow, and adopting a new mode of dress. The basic teachings of monotheism, monogamy, and holiness have never been lost, but have been overlaid by many of the ceremonies and customs of the neighboring Hindus, espe-cially in the case of birth, marriage, death, and holy days. Woman has always been held in high esteem and great honor, this being remarkable in a country like India. Today Parsic women have complete equality of status with men, even in public assemblies.

The religion of the Parsees is a universal monotheism. It imposes love of God, love of truth, and charity in all its connotations. All must strive to do some good. Their creed includes a belief in the existence of angels to assist man-kind; in the efficacy and necessity of prayer; in the immor-tality of the soul; in an afterlife of rewards and punishments. It is a pure religion with no attempt at propitiation of evil forces. Their morality is summarized in the words "holi-ness," "pure thought," "good word," and "good deed." The common virtues are extolled and inculcated. Truth is espe-cially exalted. In the end, man rests his pardon on the mercy of God and his reward on His bounty.

Although the number of true Zoroastrians today is small, this belief has left its mark on Judaism and Islam, and, through these and Mithraism, on Christianity. The Jews translated Ahriman into their Satan. From the Persians they first learned ideas of Heaven and Hell, and of a Judgment

Day. Accounts of The Affair color Judaic and Christian accounts of the last days in both the Old and the New Testaments. Mithraism, a direct outgrowth of Zoroastrianism, was adapted in large part to Christian teachings and rituals, as we shall see.

Chapter VII

Brahmanism—The Hindu Faith

EARLIEST India was animistic. There were numerous local gods, some of whom were allegorical representations of fortune, courage, health, plenty, etc. As Aryan invaders came to India they built up an elaborate ritual. This they wrote into the Vedas, or wise sayings, and tried to maintain by establishment of the caste system. Originally there were four castes—the Brahmans, or priests; the warriors; the merchants and traders; and the Sudras, or miscellaneous groups. Only the first was able to remain pure, the others being broken into many sects and subsects. The Brahmans became very rich and powerful, and through the ritual were able to control even the gods.

As the new religion moved southward to the Ganges, a new spirit of despair and longing to leave life entered man. This spirit was expressed in the Upanishads, written about 800–600 B.C. One great result was the abolition of all the old gods except the great triad of Brahma, Vishnu, and Shiva (Siva). Brahma was described as the Self-existent, the Creator, the Infinite, the It. He was too abstract for the common man and hence had no strong following except among the priests. Vishnu, the Preserver, originally a Vedic sun-god, became very popular with the masses because of his power of reincarnation. His wife typified plenty or prosperity. Shiva, the destroyer and rebuilder of life, was the most popular in spite of the fact that he promoted endurance of pain, self-mutilation, starvation, and solitary meditation. He was passionate, violent, and licentious, teaching that passion was a poison the only antidote to which was poison. This led to many orgies of eating, drinking, and sexuality. His symbol today is still the phallic symbol described in an earlier chapter, but for the modern Hindu it has lost its original sex significance. The oldest pictures of Shiva show him with trident and rosary—the second of which symbols passed first to Islam and later to Christianity from Hinduism.

Probably it is Shiva who provided the source of the Yoga mysticism which so interests some moderns. It seems certain that a spiritual trance does occur. The older philosophical explanation of this trance was that it was a glimpse of the Great Beyond. Modern psychologists explain it as more likely a sublimation of sexual desire.

The ultimate good to be aimed at the old Hindus thought to be Liberation, absorption into the It, or Nirvana—a state of mind rather than a physical state. Only by complete annihilation of the ego could the individual gain Nirvana. Death was not a release, but merely an interval between periods of conscious existence. As soon as the influence of one's good deeds was used up, he returned to the earth, by a process of transmigration, in a new form better or worse than his previous one depending on his former life. Man had to work out his own end without the direction, aid, or sympathy of a supreme being. This promoted bodily purity, unselfishness, self-restraint, and a fine sense of justice. The desire to end desire eventually led to asceticism, unorthodox thinking, and anchorite living.

One of these anchorites who for a time had considerable influence was a young prince, Mahavira, who lived circa 599–529 B.C. At the age of thirty he turned ascetic, and after twelve years of self-denial he believed he had reached Nirvana, becoming Jina, the Conqueror. From this title was derived the term Jainism. Mahavira did not believe in any gods, in the Vedas, or in prayer. He did believe in self-annihilation and the destruction of desire by will power. In his disciples he required poverty and humility. They were forbidden either to hate or to love; to harm or kill any living creature; to have any contact with women. After his death many legends sprang up about him, and within a century and a half he himself had become regarded as a god. It seems that his "Three Jewels"—Right Faith, Right Knowledge, and Right Living—were not enough for the masses, who needed gods to cling to. Jainism gradually returned to orthodoxy, and is now distinguished only by the commandment against killing.

Hinduism today is the strongest religion in India, and is still increasing its following. Most estimates place the number of Hindus at three hundred million. Hinduism is a religio-social system in which the single dominant note is caste, established by law in the Code of Manu. The castes are divided into two main sects and approximately sixty subsects, all very much more tolerant of each other than Christian sects, although they have only the caste idea in common. All adore and recognize the Brahmanic gods, who have an outward form for the crowd but a hidden inner meaning for the initiate. All accept the Brahmanic prescribed rituals; all venerate the cow; all observe rules of caste in marriage and in sharing of food; all go to the Brahmans for forms concerning birth, marriage, and death; and all accept the orthodoxy of Brahmanic scriptures.

Some of the latter contain teachings of a high moral nature. In the *Bhagavad-Gita* we find:

He who does his work for my [Vishnu's] sake, who is wholly devoted to me, who is free from attachments to earthly things, who is without hate of any being, he enters into me.

Again, from the *Dhammapada* we quote:

Those who love nothing and hate nothing have no fetters. . . . As rain breaks through an ill-thatched house, passion will break through an unreflecting mind. . . . He who possesses virtue and intelligence, who is just, speaks the truth, and does what is his own business, him will the world hold dear. . . . Health is the greatest of gifts; contentedness the best of riches; trust is the best of relationships; Nirvana the highest happiness.

Chapter VIII

Buddhism

ORIGINAL BUDDHISM : GAUTAMA BUDDHA

ANOTHER Hindu who was to become the founder of an entirely new branch of religion was Siddhartha Gautama, born about 560 B.C. Like Mahavira, he was born into riches and nobility, and spent the early part of his life in riotous living. At the age of twenty-eight he married and became the father of a son. Shortly after the birth of this son, he left behind his riches and family to seek Nirvana. He tried many ways to gain surcease and rest—philosophy, asceticism, hypnotism—but for six years could gain no ease. Then one day while sitting in meditation under a banyan tree, he caught a vision of the way of salvation. He had learned the folly of excess. From this day forward he became the Buddha, "the Enlightened One," and a new religion was born.

Buddhism had its source, like Hinduism, in the Upanishads, but rejected much Brahmanic doctrine. Gautama discounted the authority of the old Vedic laws, and discarded completely the doctrines of caste and the priesthood, theology, and ritual of the Brahmans. The Buddhist stresses moral living much more than ritualism. From the Jain, the Buddhist differs mainly in stress—Mahavira stressed salvation for the individual, Gautama for the masses. The command of Gautama, "Go ye now out of compassion for the world and preach the doctrine which is glorious" should be compared to the New Testament commandment of Christ, "Go ye into all the world and preach the gospel." Buddhism, with Islam and Christianity, is the third great missionary religion.

Pure Buddhism leaves no room for gods, priests, prayers,

temples, or ritual. Gautama taught that since Nirvana was a state of mind, it could best be reached by mental discipline. He gathered about him a small brotherhood and began to preach a new gospel of Four Elementary Truths:

1. Both birth and death bring grief, and life is vain.

2. The cause of grief, and hence of vanity of life, is indulgence of desire.

3. With the ending of desire will come surcease from grief.

4. The best way to end desire is by application of wisdom and intelligence to life.

The Buddhist argues that wherever there is individuality, there must be limitation; wherever there is limitation, there must be ignorance; wherever there is ignorance, there must be error; and wherever there is error, there must be sorrow; and that, therefore, sorrow has its source in individuality. The road to salvation, then, is spiritual self-control, which can be reached by following the Eightfold Noble Path to the goal of worthiness. The eight stages of this way are: right belief—free from superstition and delusion; right aims—high and worthy of earnest, intelligent men; right speech—truthful, open, and kindly; right conduct—peaceful, pure, and honest; right livelihood—bringing hurt or injury to no living thing; right effort toward self-knowledge, self-guidance, self-control; right thought—the active mind; and right rapture—or earnest meditation, thought, and contemplation on the deep mysteries of life. The five great obstacles to the higher life are sloth, pride, malice, lust, and doubt.

There are thirty-seven divisions of Arahatship, the state of being worthy. First are the four earnest meditations—of the body, of the senses, of the ideas, and of reason. A second group contains the fourfold Great Struggle—to prevent trouble arising, to put away erroneous ideas that have arisen, to produce goodness which did not previously exist, and to increase goodness which is already existent. A third is the fourfold Path to Iddhi: the will to acquire Iddhi, the necessary exertion to acquire it, the necessary preparation of the heart, and investigation of Iddhi—each united with earnest meditation and the struggle against evil disposition. Fourth and fifth groups have five divisions each—exercise and enjoyment of faith, energy, thought, contemplation, and wisdom. A sixth group is composed of the seven kinds of wisdom —zeal, intelligence, meditation, investigation, joy, repose, and serenity. These twenty-nine divisions, together with the Eightfold Noble Path outlined in the previous paragraph, complete the state of worthiness.

Man's salvation thus depends not upon what he is but upon what he does. Buddhism does not admit those mental or emotional qualities usually termed "soul." It is the one great religion that dispenses with an external superhuman or supernatural authority. It appeals to man to be his own reformer, ruler, and refuge. Gautama Buddha was a spiritual liberator. He, like Christ, worked to perfect and spiritualize doctrines already existent. Both Buddha and Christ tried to set men free from formal dogma that they might follow their own convictions and consciences. Buddhism is ennobling and encouraging in its teaching that man has within himself the strength and virtue which release him from dependence on the supernatural. It is the only great religion that preaches that man can trust himself.

Buddhism gives no authoritative account of the creation, nor does it even propose an "end of the world." There is no explanation of why or how death and sin entered the world. There is no promise of divine assistance. It does not offer exemption from evil and pain in return for prayer. There is no remission of sins, but expiation is required of each individual. However, since it gives men the strength to carry through evil, plus spiritual joy and enthusiasm, it must be classified as a religion and not merely as a philosophy of life.

The scripture or holy writings of the Buddhists is the Tripitaka, or "Three Baskets of the Law." These are the earliest and most authoritative accounts of Buddha's teachings. They were recited at a meeting of the disciples at Rajagaha shortly after the death of the Master by three of the leading apostles. They continued in oral form until the time of Asoka in 242 B.C. when they were committed to writing. Just as four of Christ's disciples are credited with the Gospels, so three of Gautama's disciples are credited with the Pitakas.

The first, or Abidharma Pitaka, was given by Kasyapa, and is made up of metaphysical and philosophical doctrines. The second is the book of the law and regulations of discipline, known as the Vinaya Pitaka, the work of Upali. Here are found three sets of rules of conduct for perfecting the mind —one set for those who would be blameless, a second for those who would be virtuous, and a third for those who choose to be perfect. According to the first set, the blameless man must follow the ordinary moral laws of purity and freedom from cruelty, deeds of violence, and covetousness. In the second set, the virtuous man finds that he must avoid all idle talk and renounce worldly ambition, unprofitable amusements, and luxurious tastes. The third set of laws explains that the perfect, or truly religious, man lives for the mind and spirit only. He must withdraw from society, be no diviner of dreams or utterer of spells, make no prophecies, practice no astrology, lay claim to no miraculous or healing power. His work must be only in the intellectual and spiritual spheres. Also in the Vinaya Pitaka are found the Buddhist Ten Commandments, which should be compared with the Mosaic tables in the Old Testament. They are divided into two groups, the first five for all Buddhists, the second five required only of members of the Samga:—

1. Thou shalt not kill any living being.
2. Thou shalt not take that which is not thine.
3. Thou shalt not commit adultery.
4. Thou shalt not prevaricate, but shall speak the word of truth.
5. Thou shalt not partake of intoxicating liquors.
6. Thou shalt not partake of food after midday.
7. Thou shalt not be present at any dramatic, dancing, or musical performance.
8. Thou shalt not use any personal adornment or any perfume.
9. Thou shalt not sleep on a broad, comfortable bed.
10. Thou shalt not be owner of any gold or silver.

The third, or Sutta Pitaka, was given by Ananda, who has been called the "St. John of Buddhism." Here are expounded many of the parables and sermons of Gautama. To quote:

Well-makers have the water where they wish; fletchers bend the arrow; carpenters shape the log of wood; the wise man fashions himself. . . . If one man conquer in battle a thousand times ten thousand men, and another conquer himself, the latter is the greater victor. . . . This is the beginning: watch over the senses, have restraint under the law, keep noble friends whose life is pure and who are not slothful, dwell constantly on the highest thoughts.

Buddhism did not spread rapidly until the time of Asoka in the third century, who sent missionaries throughout India. This religion had a powerful appeal to the poor. As time went on, Buddhism depreciated from a high moral system to a theological dogma with Gautama a god, and Nirvana a post-mortem heaven. Much paganism and alien ritual was added—Shinto in Japan, Taoism in China. From Christianity, the Buddhist adopted the cross, the miter, the holy-water font, and the censer. There are now extant many pictures of the Earth Mother Isis nursing the infant Gautama just as Mary holds Jesus. Pure, original Buddhism today is found only in Siam, Ceylon, and Burma.

CHINESE BUDDHISM

Chinese Buddhism should not be confused with the system given by Gautama, as it is a distinct offshoot. It entered China by way of Persia, not India, and was simply added to the older beliefs. It was attractive to the people because it had an idolized god and a whole new scheme of temple architecture. It was a religion of salvation, offering much comfort in a life after death. Some of the fundamental features of the system were its appeal to the conscience, its vast scope for present and future, its belief in a Merciful One, and its belief in the future rest in Paradise. It taught to avoid evil and do good, to banish lust and impure desire from the heart, and to progress in the way of righteousness.

The Chinese worked out an elaborate system of the universe. The gods, thirty-three in number, lived on the summit of the Divine Mountains, much as the Greek pantheon lived on Mount Olympus or as the Norse gods lived in Asgard. The number thirty-three derived from very ancient times when Chronos (Time) ruled the world, and the year, the four seasons, and each day of the lunar month of twenty-eight days was represented as a god. Above this home of the gods were three higher heavens, one above the other. The lowest of these was the Kama Heaven abounding in earthly pleasures. Above this was the Rupa Heaven, which had forms but no earthly pleasures. Highest of all was the Arupa Heaven, wherein were neither forms nor any human conceptions. Under the earth were three earth-prisons or hells, the lowest being a burning hell with iron walls similar to Homer's Tartarus. In these prisons the wicked were confined for long but not endless periods. In addition to this multiple system there was a Western Paradise, a place of golden streets, exquisite birds, gorgeous flowers, and palaces wherein dwelt only happy people.

Today in China, Confucianism is the religion of the learned classes, and all civil service examinations are based on its nine books, but the loved religions of the people are the warmer, kindlier, more promising, and more hopeful Taoism and Buddhism.

Chapter IX

Religions in the Far East

EARLIEST records in China reveal an advanced animism which was almost monotheistic. Their symbol for the Supreme Being signifies "Great One," and is often translated "Heaven." This approach to monotheism was disfigured and hidden under a mass of superstition. Worship was usually associated with the more prominent objects of nature such as the sun, the moon, or a river.

There were two sacrificial rituals. One belonged to the religion of the state, and was directed toward the Supreme Being. Since there never was a priest class in ancient China, the only performer in this rite was the emperor, and the sacrifice was usually annual. The other sacrificial service was addressed to the spirits of the dead, and any father could perform these rites. The sacrifice was for purposes of prayer and thanksgiving. Since this second rite belonged to the people, devotion to the dead became the keynote of Chinese belief. Although ancestor worship did uphold prosperity of the ancient system and first lead China into civilization, still it acted as a bar to progress because it was backward-looking.

Filial piety led to burying food and servants in allegory with the deceased—probably in actuality at an earlier date. There was no attempt to deify the dead, and never a prayer for the dead, as that would be an insult to one's ancestors. The sacrifice was simply an act of honor. This rite shows a belief in the continued existence of the spirits of men after death, but the religion maintained strict silence on the kind of existence it was, especially for the wicked. Good and ill acts of the parents were thought to be rewarded and punished in the children—a doctrine that should be compared to the Judaic teaching of reward and punishment "even to the third generation."

TAOISM

One of the great Chinese religious founders was Lao-tse, born just at the opening of the sixth century B.C. The sixth was an important century for advance of religious ideas, for it produced Lao-tse, Confucius, Gautama, Mahavira, and Zoroaster. The followers of Lao-tse became known as *Taoists*, and the belief as *Taoism*. It was originally a high, aloof religion with no gods, prayers, priests, or sacrifice—really a high-toned philosophy. When a very old man, Lao-tse summarized his teachings in a five-thousand-word treatise which was destined to become the Taoist Bible, bearing the title *Tao-Teh-King*. It is divided into two sections, the first of which explains the *why* of the universe, the second, the *how* of life.

Tao originally meant "Road" or "Way," but later came to signify the fundamental reality, the doctrine, or the perfect Something. *Teh* was man's single virtue, to emulate the poise of Tao. Thus the *Tao-Teh-King* was the "Book of the Doctrine of Reason and Virtue." Taoism inculcated goodness, simplicity, spontaneity, purity, and gentleness in everyday life.

Lao-tse said, "Recompense injury with kindness. There are three things which I grasp as precious: the first is Compassion, the second Moderation, and the third is Modesty or Humility." These three things became known as the "Three Jewels of Taoism," which differed from Confucianism mainly in the first of these. While Confucius taught reciprocity, Lao-tse taught to return good for evil—and this more than five hundred years before the time of Christ.

We gain our best accounts of early Taoism from some of the early writers. One of these, Chuang-tse, described Tao as follows:

It is all pervasive; it fills the universe with sublime grandeur; it causes the sun and moon to revolve in their orbits; it gives life to the most microscopic insect. In itself formless, it is the source of all form; inaudible, it is the source of all sound; invisible, it is the origin of all sight; inactive, it produces and sustains every phenomenon. It is impartial, impersonal, and passionless.

Again, we quote the opening from one of the Taoist books, *The Book of Recompense:*

Advance in all that is in harmony with good; retreat from all that is opposed to it. Walk not in the paths of depravity, nor deceive yourselves by sinning in the dark where none can see you. Accumulate virtue, and store up merit; treat all with love and gentleness; be loyal; be dutiful; be respectful to your elders and kind to your juniors; be upright yourselves in order that you may reform others; pity the orphan and the widow; reverence the aged, cherish the young; do not injure even insects, grass, or trees. When a man gains his desires, let it be as though his good fortune were your own; when one suffers loss, as though you suffered it yourself. Never publish the failings of another, or make a parade of your own merits; put a stop to evil, and afford every encouragement to goodness. When you are reviled, cherish no resentment; be kind and generous without seeking any return.

A teaching so aloof could not hold the common man. The disciples who followed made it a ritual only, and used the *Tao-Teh-King* as a source book of magic. For a long period they searched for the elixir of life and the philosopher's stone. By the middle of the second century B.C. Lao-tse himself had been deified, and was worshipped with sacrifice. Modern Taoism is a system of unreasoning credulity based on superstition, a foolish idolatry served by an ignorant and venal priesthood.

CONFUCIANISM

K'ung Fu-tse ("Our Master Kung") is better known by the Latin form of his name, Confucius. He was born in the middle of the sixth century, in 551 B.C., a descendant of the Shang dynasty. He was a son by his father's second marriage. The father died soon after Confucius was born, and the latter lived in poverty with his mother until her death when he was twenty-three. Married in his early twenties, Confucius remained monogamous throughout his life and became the father of a son and two daughters.

As a teacher, he demanded only a small fee but ardent desire from his pupils. Holding a minor civil service post, he once had occasion to visit the capital, where he met and talked with Lao-tse. When middle-aged he became governor of a town, and was so successful that he received rapid promotion to become magistrate of a state. This state, under his government, came so near to being a model state, that his superiors became jealous and he was dismissed from office. For many years after this (496 B.C.) he wandered about the country homeless and in want. In the spring of 478 B.C. he died, aged seventy-three years. He arose one morning, walked about his garden, reentered the house and spoke to a disciple of a dream he had had presaging his death: "The great mountain must crumble, the strong beam must break, the wise man must wither away like a plant." He took to his bed and died a week later.

He was not a founder, but rather a sage of simple, practical wisdom. Not a religious man, he was a student of ancient beliefs who conserved and passed on this knowledge. He never claimed to be more than a man, nor did he claim any supernatural endowment, but felt himself to have a mission inspired by love of mankind. He was a closer parallel to the Hebrew Solomon of the Old Testament than to any of the founders of religions. He stressed regularity in everyday living, advocated temperance in eating and drinking, frequently discussed rules of propriety, stressed the importance of learning, loyalty, ethics, and truthfulness, and urged caution in fasting, making war, and treatment of disease.

His highest contribution was in the field of ethics. In society he perceived five relationships, and outlined the proprieties to be observed in each—between husband and wife, parent and child, elders and youth, rulers and subjects, friend and friend. He formulated a Golden Rule of reciprocity, "What you do not want done to yourself, do not to others," but never advanced as far as Lao-tse or Christ, both of whom taught to return good for evil.

After his death his sayings were collected and written down in the Analects, from which we quote a few choice proverbs:

Learning without thought is labor lost; thought without learning is perilous. . . . It is only the truly virtuous who can love or hate others. . . . To be poor without murmuring is difficult; to be rich without pride is easy. . . . The superior man is catholic and not a partisan—he does what is proper to the position in which he is, he does not desire to go beyond it.

Confucius received the post-mortem honor of being raised to Imperial rank, and in 1907 he became one of the prime deities of China, ranking with the deities of Heaven and Earth. Today his teachings are the basis for education and all civil service examinations in China.

SHINTO

Shinto, the national religion of Japan, is not really a religion at all, but it is the oldest and one of the simplest of creeds. It arose out of hero worship, the essential principle being ancestor worship. *Shinto* means, "Way of the Spirits."

It is a religio-political system which has neither sacred books nor a moral code; which extends only to the subjects of the Mikado; which recognizes no distinction between its mythology and the history of the nation; which treats of no future state and knows neither a paradise nor a hell; and which embraces the Imperial Dynasty of Japan as a part of its godhead, thus giving the Emperor divine right to rule his subjects. It has four distinctive emblems. The first of these is the bird's rest, consisting of two upright barked unpainted tree trunks with another resting on their top with a horizontal beam below. The second is the *gohei*, a slim wand of unpainted wood, with two long pieces of paper notched alternately on opposite sides of it. The third and fourth are both of legendary origin: the mirror and the rope of rice straw.

The central shrine of Shinto is at Ise, in central Japan, and pilgrimages are made here. These pilgrimages are an excuse for a great merrymaking, ending in all the vicious attractions of the near-by city of Yamada with its saloons and brothels. Deities are numberless. The best that can be said of Shinto is that there were never bloody sacrifices or cruel or immoral rituals. It has no appeal to any instinct of good or evil; and it is hollow and empty, promising no definite destiny. What its future will be since Emperor Hirohito has renounced his claim to divinity is uncertain.

Chapter X

The Mystery Cults—Mithraism

In the Western world from the fifth century B.C. on there was increasing doubt concerning the old gods. The influx of mystery religions from the East, the Sophist movement, and discovery of natural laws all had their effect on reducing the importance of the old Olympic Pantheon. New philosophies—those of Epicureans and Stoics particularly—brought new beliefs and new explanations of life. As the old gods carried little moral effectiveness and promised but little hope for the future, they lost ground before the mystery religions with their promises of better things to come. In Greece, the Dionysus and Demeter cults were prominent. In Rome, the Earth Mother Attis or Isis cult had many followers—traces of Isis worship are found as far west as the Seine River in France. This was the period when the "oracles" flourished, especially the one at Delphi.

According to legends concerning this oracle, there came from "the bowels of the earth" a vapor which emerged through an orifice in the rock floor of the temple to Apollo at Delphi. A priestess inhaled these vapors, passed into a trance, and then forecast the future—usually in some rid-dling fashion much as would a modern seer at a spiritual-istic seance. One of the most famous answers was given to Croesus, King of Lydia, when he asked the oracle if he should make war on Persia. The oracle gave answer: "If you do so, you will destroy a mighty empire." Misinterpreting this answer, Croesus declared war, thereby bringing about the destruction of his own mighty empire.

One of the most significant answers was given to a question as to who was the wisest man of the Greeks. The answer was the single word "Socrates." Socrates, himself a religious man, doubted the validity of the answer and devoted the rest of his life (unsuccessfully) to the search for a wiser man. His unshakable conviction was that the human mind by application could determine value, right, virtue, beauty, and other great ideals. He believed that the state could be improved by cultivating the individual. He made no attempt to bring forth a new religion, but he became the nucleus of a philosophical school which was to produce Aristotle and Plato. Late in life he was tried for corruption of youth and executed. In death he was more powerful than in life, as the serenity of his end had profound influence on the Greek world and, through it, on modern thought.

The later Greeks, with a developing sense of right and wrong, reinterpreted the old gods as moral beings. Many of the old religious stories became mere folk legends of the people. A belief in a hereafter led to a belief in a Judgment Day with rewards and punishments. The old Hades, where souls of all the dead had gone according to ancient myth, became a place of torment for the wicked guarded by the great mastiff, Cerberus. The initiate and the acceptable ones passed to bliss in the Elysian Fields, formerly reserved for heroes.

One of the earliest forms, and one of the most popular, arising with belief in a future life was Chthonian worship. The Chthonians believed that man felt the same wants, pains, and pleasures in the future life as in the present; that he had the same property rights; that he had the same need for wife, cook, horse, tools, etc. The main difference was an increase in his power to do harm. The eldest son succeeded to be master, priest, and king in his father's household, and on him fell the duty of burial with appropriate rites. Woe fell on the son who failed in this duty. Gradually the family became extended to include the clan or tribe. As a man was under the protection of his gods only "at home," it is easy to understand the terrible fear of banishment shown by the ancients. Their religion touched neither heart nor conscience, and this explains their moral code. Acts which seem to us political were to them religious. Every war was a holy war because it was against people with different gods. There was no moral obligation to captives, who might be sold, enslaved, or slain. Even the early Roman census was for religious purposes, to ensure that all attended the lustration of atonement for previous shortcomings of the state.

Many cults arose in Greece and Rome, involving myths and legends of the birth, adventures, death, and resurrection of a youth representative of the sun, life, or light. Many of the old "heroes"—Bellerophon, Mercury, Perseus, Theseus, Cephalus, Apollo, Hercules, Osiris—filled the places of chief importance in these cults. Another group was centered on the prolific Earth Mother, and of these the Isis cult was most far-flung. The Romans would have made a cult of Jesus if they could, and they did add much of the ritual of their most popular cult, Mithraism, to Christianity.

As the old cults died out, that of Mithras gained in importance. Purer and more ethical than other mysteries, it was particularly attractive to the Roman soldier and the intelligentsia. The cult was introduced to Rome about the middle of the first century, and flourished throughout the second and third centuries, becoming a serious threat and rival of Christianity in the whole Western world. Originally a Persian deity (cf. chapter on Zoroastrianism), Mithras was supposed to have been born of a virgin, the birth being witnessed by only a few shepherds. Ahura Mazda had made him the deity of truth and light, a sun-god equal in majesty to the Supreme Being himself, and his chief supporter in the fight against Ahriman, the spirit of evil. His life reached its climax in the great bullfight, a struggle against a great bull allegorically representing the forces of darkness. By slaying the bull and letting its blood, Mithras symbolically fructified the earth.

As Mithraism moved westward it proved a fertile ground for the addition of mystic meaning. Practically all of the symbolism of Osiris was added to the Mithraic cultus, even to the fact that Isis became the virgin mother of Mithras. The Persian distaste for idols was lost during the western exodus, and we find many idols in the West. A common element of Mithraism was that its rites were carried on in caves (either natural or artificial). They believed that on the Day of Judgment all nonbelievers would perish and that the initiate would inherit the world in peace forever.

Since Mithras was a sun-god, Sunday was automatically sacred to him—the "Lord's Day"—long before Christ. On

December 25th, just after the winter solstice, there were elaborate rituals and celebrations. Bells were rung, hymns were sung, candles lit, gifts given, sacraments of bread and water administered to the initiate. Between December 25th and the spring equinox (Easter, from *Eastra*, the Latin form of Astarte) came the mystical forty days' search for Osiris (cf. chapter on Egypt), which later was the origin for Christian Lent. On Black Friday (cf. Good Friday) the taurobolium, or bull-slaying, was represented. At this festival, the sacrament often comprised blood drinking. Mithras, worn out by the battle, was symbolically represented by a stone image lain on a bier as a corpse. He was mourned for in liturgy, and placed in a sacred rock tomb called "Petra," from which he was removed *after three days* in a great festival of rejoicing.

Initiation into the Mithraic mystery was an elaborate ritual probably lasting twelve days, as remains of monuments show twelve episodes. This initiation was no simple process but sometimes involved painful trials by fire, water, hunger, thirst, cold, scourging, bleeding, branding, and mock menace of death. A sacrament of bread and water was given (water was used before wine in the Christian sacrament). There seems to be no historical evidence for the tales of fearfulness in these rites or for any licentiousness being involved. There was never any question of their being both moral and consolatory.

With these august rituals and promise of immortality, it is easy to understand why this cult spread quickly throughout Europe. The Mithraists became Christians easily, for whereas Mithras was always soluble into a mysterious abstraction, Christ was literally humanized; and in religion the concrete always carries more force than the abstract. There were many points of similarity in the two religions; and where differences did appear, the Christian often absorbed the Mithraic ritual. They had the same holy day (Sunday), similar Christmas and Easter festivals, a similar sacrament in the mass, and many instances of similarity in vocabulary and litany. Both Mithras and Christ were described variously as "the Way," "the Truth," "the Light," "the Life," "the Word," "the Son of God," "the Good Shepherd." The Christian litany to Jesus could easily be an

allegorical litany to the sun-god. Mithras is often represented as carrying a lamb on his shoulders, just as Jesus is.
Midnight services were found in both religions. The virgin
mother Isis was easily merged with the virgin mother Mary.
Petra, the sacred rock of Mithraism, became Peter, the foundation of the Christian Church. (Cf. the New Testament,
Matt. 16:18: "Thou art Peter, and upon this rock I will build
my church.") The robe of Mithras, absorbed from the older
Osiris cult, was always described as in one piece representing universal light, and may be the source for the seamless
robe of Christ worn at the time of the Crucifixion.

Thus was the way made easier for the spread of Christianity. It had all the beauty of ritual and liturgy of the
ancient cults, but brought a new warmth unknown to the
earlier religions.

Chapter XI

Mohammed, "The Praised One"

ARABIA was destined to produce one of the world's greatest religions, a belief which was to attract over four hundred million followers. Early Arabia was divided into three sections—Sheba, Nejd, and Hejaz. There was no political unity, most of the people being nomads, with only a few merchants and artisans. The latter practiced their trades and skills in small villages around the holy places. Tribal warfare was common, but it was broken by the four sacred months in fall and spring when fighting was forbidden. During these periods pilgrims could make their way across the desert unmolested to pay their respects at the holy shrine of the Kaaba in Mecca. The Kaaba still stands—now a Mohammedan shrine. It is almost cubical in shape and is now covered with a black cloth which is renewed annually by the Egyptian government, the old covering being cut into small pieces and sold as relics. In the Kaaba was a most highly venerated black stone of meteoric origin. This shrine was the single unifying influence among the Arabian tribes before Mohammed.

The people were openhanded and hospitable, as all nomads are, faithful in their agreements and loving freedom, poetry, and courage. To the stranger they were fierce and unscrupulous except in the holy months. Many deities were worshipped and much paganism was to be found, interspersed with Jewish and Christian communities.

In Mecca, the Holy City, the Koreish were the chief tribe; and a single clan, the Banu Hashim, had risen to prominence because of so simple a thing as monopoly of the drinking-water supply for pilgrims. Into this clan in 570 A.D. was born Ubu'l-Kassim, later to become known as Mohammed, "the Praised One," just as Gautama became known as Buddha, "the Enlightened One," or Jesus became known as Christ, "the Anointed One." His father died shortly after his birth, and his mother when he was six years old; so he was raised by his grandfather and his uncle Abu-Talib. The latter he followed on expeditions of trade and war. Although he had no schooling, contacts made at this time with the learning and religions of the Near East and Egypt were later to influence him greatly.

In appearance he was not remarkable, but he was comely. Of medium height and build, he had dark, slightly curly hair and rather large extremities—head, hands, and feet. The heavy eyebrows over the dark eyes indicated the thoughtful man that he was. His friends tell of a black vein which swelled out on his forehead when he was angered. Extremely neat and cleanly, he had a particular aversion for strong odors of all kinds. Amiable and companionable, he was respected highly by his neighbors for the wisdom and pertinence of his conversation. All accounts of his life mention the truth, sincerity, and fidelity of the man. He was not noted for personal courage, but nevertheless showed bravery and coolness in danger. Unable to read or write, he yet possessed a keen insight into the psychology of human nature. From middle life on he suffered from nervous disorders which caused lividity, foaming at the mouth, fits of unconsciousness, fever, and fierce headaches.

He became apprenticed as camel-boy to a rich widow, Khadija. In her employ he rose to be manager of her trading interests, doing so well that she eventually married him. Although she was much older than he, the marriage was a success. Mohammed remained faithful to her until her death and always spoke with reverence of her memory, holding her in much higher esteem than any of his later wives. Known as a good father and stepfather, he was not yet an outstanding man in his community.

The marriage with Khadija made Mohammed financially independent. There was now more leisure time for meditation and thought. In his trading journeys he had gathered ideas of monotheism from Jews and Christians, and ideas of asceticism from the latter. From one of his lonely vigils in the desert he returned with the firm conviction that the angel Gabriel had appeared to him in a vision and summoned him as the prophet who was to proclaim the doctrine of a single universal god, Allah, to his people. He taught the uselessness of idols, and the doctrine of *Islam*, or submission to a single reality, *Allah akbar* ("God is great"). He began to prophesy a Day of Judgment, with a future of rewards and punishments. Islam is largely based on Christianity, but should not be judged as an offshoot of this other great religion.

He had few converts at first—in three years only thirteen followers including Khadija and his close friends. When he began to proclaim the new faith openly, he evoked the ire of the priests of the Kaaba, who were the keepers of the idols. His own tribe, the Koreish, gave his followers the despised title of *Muslims*, or *Moslems*, meaning "traitors"— but the name was to survive with the new meaning of "the reconciled ones," or "those who submit to Allah."

The priests could not fight him openly in Mecca because of a tabu against bloodshed in the Holy City. However, the rulers attempted to starve him and his followers into submission. He fled to the neighboring town of Taif; but, making no converts there, he begged for permission to return to Mecca. This permission was granted on condition that he would not preach to the Meccans. This condition he observed in the letter, but persisted in preaching to traders, aliens, and pilgrims in the market place. He was an inspirational preacher, teaching that man should submit to the will of a loving Allah, that he should treat his fellow as a brother, that he should be kind, considerate, and charitable. He told slightly revised versions of the biblical tales of Ibrahim, Suleiman, and Jesus; of a paradise for all believers; of a devil's hell.

On the night of July 16, 622, an attempt was made to assassinate Mohammed in spite of the law against bloodshed in the Holy City. Some converts had been made in neighboring Yathrib, and so Mohammed and the Moslems moved to that town. Mohammed arrived there September 20th. This flight became known in history as the "Hegira," and marks the beginning of the Mohammedan era. The first work on arriving in their new home was to build a mosque for prayer. Hoping to win Jewish converts Mohammed at first gave the order to face Jerusalem for prayers, but failing in his purpose he ordered all to face Mecca. His first attempts to win converts were by preaching and persuasion. As this did not bring great results, he resorted to a mild, well-established form of religious trickery—the addition of some pagan rituals—with considerable success.

Partly because he needed funds and partly because his followers were not skilled in agriculture as were the natives of Yathrib, he organized fighting bands to raid caravans. Having no ties with the older religions, he sent them out even in the peace months. This started Arabia's Holy War. Mohammed's whole movement took on the character of religious militarism. He made the Moslems fanatic fighters by teaching that admission to Paradise was assured for all those who died fighting in the cause of Allah. After his first successes, the name Yathrib was changed to Medina, the "City of the Prophet." By 631, all Arabia, including Mecca, had been conquered. He returned to Mecca as the Holy City, and died there the following year. He had brought a new unity, both political and social, to the Arabs, which was to result in their becoming a world power.

The desert tribes, fired with religious zeal, now spread Islam from India to Spain. Egypt, Syria, Asia Minor, North Africa, Spain, and Constantinople fell before the advance of the Moslem Empire. The victory over the Arabs at Tours, France, in 732 by Charles Martel was all that prevented the conquest of Europe. How different might have been the history of Western Europe had the Moslems conquered! The "hunger urge" of discontented masses had added to the impetus of religious fanaticism. In their advance they had unwittingly strengthened the Roman Papacy by destruction of the patriarchates of Alexandria, Jerusalem, and Antioch; by removal of the Bishop of Carthage; and by weakening the patriarchate at Constantinople.

The Caliphs, or "Successors," unified this great new empire. Their function was fourfold—religious, military, judicial, and political. They produced a centralized government on the old Persian pattern with a vizier over the whole empire and emirs over each province, all directly responsible to the Caliph. In 762 a new capital was set up at Bagdad, which became a center of learning and science. The teachings of Mohammed were here compiled to make the Koran.

As the Empire spread, beautiful mosques, temples, and palaces were built—remains can still be seen at Cordova, Granada, and Seville in Spain. Their learning and science were far more advanced than those of the Franks, and in so far as culture is concerned, the view taken by many of the "great victory" at Tours may be entirely erroneous.

The Koran, "the thing to be read," was entirely the work of Mohammed. Since he himself could neither read nor write, it was dictated to scribes. Supposed to be a divine revelation sent from Heaven at various times over a long period, it is contradictory in parts. It sets a high standard of law and practice: "Blessed are they who are blameless as respects women, who are charitable, who talk not vainly, who are humble, who observe their pledges and covenants, who guard their prayers." In the original it is a rhythmic chant, and it loses much of its charm in translation. Throughout, it reveals religious resignation, trust in God, nobility of ideals, charitableness to mankind, hope under adversity, and a high conception of Divine Being. The sincerity of the work is its chief merit. Mohammed, as the oracle of God, spoke with passionate earnestness and enthusiasm. In places there are such pathos, devotion, rhetoric, and imagery as to make it the finest literary work in Arabic.

The contents of the Koran, as assembled at Bagdad, are divided into three sections. In the first are found laws and precepts for the regulation of religious and civil life. Here are found the rules relating to prayer, fasting, pilgrimage, charity, property, marriage, and justice. The Moslem judges decide all cases by reference to the Koran. The second section contains histories and fables which closely parallel the Old Testament narratives. The third section contains admonitions to, and threats of Hell for, all unbelievers. Here the duties of industry, temperance, and justice are outlined. All of its twenty-nine chapters are required reading for the Moslems.

Islam has been defined as "Judaism plus missionary endeavor, or Christianity minus the teaching of St. Paul." Its ethics when practiced are literally the Sermon on the Mount translated into daily life. In its origin, it has a common source with Christianity and Judaism. The primary doctrine is that there is but one god, Allah, and that Mohammed is his prophet. Mohammed tried, but failed, to become the Jewish Messiah. His conception of Allah is borrowed entirely from Jewish sources—a creator and judge who has predestined all things and who is opposed by the Devil and his demons. Mohammed's revelations were produced from trances, like those of a modern spiritualist medium; and they may well have been reflections of Judaism and Christianity, with both of which he was thoroughly familiar. In one place in the Koran we read, "God alone is; God alone has power; He made us; He can kill us and keep us alive." The good believer tries to "walk with God" or have him present in his daily life. The Muslims are not slaves to priests, having no need of an intermediary to intercede with Allah for them. They kneel and pray wherever they happen to be at prayer time. The outward signs of Islam are charity, prayer, fasting, and the pilgrimage to Mecca. Minimum alms is one-fortieth of income, but 10 per cent is not unusual. Fasting is in essence a discipline, but it has a value for health. The pilgrimage is required of all true believers and is thus a bond of union which results in a Mohammedan Church.

The reality of a Day of Judgment with an afterlife of rewards and punishments was emphasized. At death, it was thought, the soul of the believer was lifted from his body and shown a ledger of all his deeds. If pious, the soul passed to Heaven to await Judgment Day. The soul of the sinner or of the unbeliever was torn from his body to await Judgment Day in Hell. Both Heaven and Hell were sensual, and were pictured as we should expect a desert people to picture them. Hell was a gulf of fire, where the sinner, wearing a cloak of fire and having only scalding water and pus for solace, could neither escape nor perish, but must suffer continous beating with maces. Heaven, reserved for followers of the Koran and those slain in battle, was a beautiful green garden of bliss. Here the soul of the believer, dressed in green robes, lolled on green cushions, enjoying forgiveness, fruit, wine with no headache in it, and service by beautiful maidens (described as "black-eyed, well-rounded of hip, but modest withal"). Here was found no sin, no regret, no foolishness, but only the greeting, "Peace! Peace!" At the Day of Judgment, the souls of all sinners were to be annihilated, the souls of unbelievers to be cast into Hell and burned and tormented forever, but the souls of the good Moslems to be restored to dwell on a paradisiac earth forever.

The marriage practices of the Mohammedans have been widely, and probably unduly, condemned. Monogamy is the general rule, although limited polygamy up to four wives is permitted provided that all wives are treated equally. Mohammed himself was celibate before at the age of twenty-five he married Khadija, and he took no other wife until her death. The numerous wives in his last few years of life were probably the result of charity to protect widows of his followers—certainly not the result of sensuality. The marriage contract requires the attestation of two witnesses and constitutes a religious act, although not a sacrament. At the time of marriage, a dowry is named by the woman which must be paid to her in the event of a divorce. When quarrels arise, arbitration by two people chosen by those concerned is resorted to, and only on advice of these arbitrators is divorce allowed. Polygamy provides for a surplus of women and serves as a check on prostitution and a protection against illegitimacy, for the child of a concubine slave inherits equally with other children. To the Moslems, adultery is a very serious offense, and is punishable for both sexes equally, by one hundred lashes delivered publicly. Women were formerly segregated, but there is considerable relaxation of this rule today. Celibacy is very rare, there being few bachelors or spinsters in Moslem society.

Mohammed permitted some pagan indulgences to creep in, but these were closely curtailed. Islam is a rigorous religion, free from cant, pride, and false humility. It advocates justice in revenge, and is a perfect equalizer of men. The Moslem is ordered to keep his contracts, aid the poor, honor his parents, protect the orphan, give good weight and fair measure, avoid waste, avoid all strong drink, and be truly humble. He has five definite religious duties:

1. Daily recitation of the Creed: "There is no God but Allah, and Mohammed is his prophet."

2. Prayer, after proper ablutions, five times daily—before and after sunset, at the day's close, before sunrise, and just after noon—facing toward Mecca, kneeling, with forehead to the ground.

3. Charity, at least one-fortieth of income, now converted to a tax used to care for the poor, to carry on religious warfare, to maintain the mosques, and to spread Islam.

4. Fasting, throughout the holy month Ramadan (compare Christian Lent), when no smoking, eating, or drinking is permitted between sunrise and sunset. During this month Gabriel was thought to have brought down the Koran from Heaven and to have delivered it to Mohammed.

5. Pilgrimage, at least once during the lifetime, to Mecca, where the Moslem must circle the Kaaba seven times, each time kissing the sacred black stone.

Mohammedan worship has remained simple—no ritual, no ecclesiastical hierarchy, no priesthood, no altars or images, no sacraments, no holy days. Some paganism has crept in, but to no greater extent than in some Christian sects— saint worship, the use of the rosary (adopted from Siva, with ninety-nine beads for the ninety-nine names of Allah, "the Unnameable"), and oblations (masses) for the dead. A public service, consisting of prayers, readings from the Koran, genuflexion, prostration, and a discourse, is held each Friday at noon. All are expected to attend, but there has been no attempt to make it a Sabbath. Colored tiles, mosaics, fine carved woodwork, rich rugs, and beautifully emblazoned pages from the Koran are used to adorn the mosques; but the use of paintings, statuary, and music is forbidden. The mosques are used not alone for worship, but also as lecture halls and schools. From their minarets, the muezzin calls to prayer at the appointed times.

Islam is a great religion, a high and noble faith. We must not lose Mohammed the prophet in looking at Mohammed the history-maker and organizer. He left a code of ethics which was a tremendous step forward for his time. Islam became one of the world's great civilizing forces. It stopped infanticide of girls, restricted slavery, and imposed a kindlier treatment of slaves. It opposed drunkenness and gambling, almost ended tribal feuds, and limited free polygamy. It advanced women's rights by restricting divorce, and imposed severe penalties for prostitution. It extended religious tolerance to the sister faiths of Christianity and Judaism, and gave to the Arabs an ideal of unity. Among the Moslems today we find no taverns, no brothels, no gaming houses, no profanity. Modern Islam has seventy-two sects with some animosity among them, but nothing like the fierce bitterness and intolerance found among Christian sects. Islam today is followed by one-fifth of mankind, and is continually making new converts. For the Arab, it was a birth from darkness to light.

Chapter XII

Jesus Christ and the Beginnings of Christianity

THE great Greek philosophers—Socrates, Plato, Aristotle, Zeno, Epicurus—had a profound effect on religions. The ancient gods declined in importance after their time. Greater freedom of conscience became the rule. Oriental mystery religions were easily introduced, and, as we have seen, they became very prolific. Into such an era came Christianity, with all the advantages and most of the attributes of the other Eastern religions, and a higher ethic than any of them.

Christianity had in common with the mystery cults the idea that man could "get right with God." There was a Saviour God who had become a man to teach mankind a way of life, who had died, who had been resurrected, and through whom those who had faith would be saved. Christianity offered greater consolation and held out the promise of a more exalted and beautiful future existence than did any other religion. It was more moral and decent, and had the advantage that the Saviour God had lived closer to the times. Much that was pagan, Oriental, or foreign to Christianity was adapted in whole or in part to the new religion. From the East came conventional architecture, the mosaic arrangements of figures, the use of the halo and incense (it was due to the use of these Eastern attributes that the Christian Church eventually broke in two—the Roman Church and the Greek Church). From Judaism Christianity adopted the idea of the fatherhood of God and the brotherhood of man, and the idea of Christian love, mercy, and justice. From the Greeks came many philosophical ideas—"the Word," "the Logos," "the Godhead." To the Greek, words had the same attributes as gods, for they could be used over and over without ever wearing out, but rather growing in strength and meaning with use. The Roman contribution was late in coming, but not less important—Romans gave organization.

The historicity of Jesus is not definitely established, but the probability is that he is a historical character. Although the Christian era dates from the supposed time of his birth, there is some evidence of error in this date. He was born during the time of Augustus, probably about 4 B.C., in the town of Bethlehem in Judaea. The first thirty years of his life may have been spent in Nazareth at the carpenter's bench of Joseph; hence the term "Nazarene" which is often applied to him. Modern archaeology lends some support to the belief that he spent a large part of this time in travel and study in the Far East. After this period he was possessed with an ideal vision of divine fatherhood and thus human brotherhood and, upon the imprisonment of one John, "the Baptist," he set out to preach and prophesy. It was now the time of Tiberius, and there were two ways for the Hebrews to show their defiance to the grinding of the Roman heel. One was by arms, the other by faith. To the group advocating the latter Jesus belonged.

Much of his teaching was based on the Rabbinical writings, both ancient and contemporary, but he brought a new form of homely metaphor and parable to his preaching. He spoke as one having authority rather than as an interpreter. His eloquence attracted a great following; and although he never claimed to be the Jewish Messiah, he was hailed by many as such. He prophesied, like a modern social reformer, a new world millennium free from misery, want, suffering, and death. Feeling himself free from custom and law, he evoked the ire of the higher Jewish classes—the scribes, Sadducees, and Pharisees. On a trumped-up charge of political conspiracy, they had Jesus tried before the Roman governor, Pontius Pilate. Although Pilate found the evidence against him to be inadequate, the Hebrews desired his end so much that he was condemned and crucified. Following the execution, his disciples dispersed and for a time no more was heard of this sect, but the cross was destined to become a symbol of love rather than of disgrace.

Jesus tried to exhibit an ideal individual as well as an ideal state. In essence, prophet though he was, he taught men to do "the will of God," to follow the Golden Rule in all relations with their fellows, to be merciful and compassionate to all. His teaching, based mainly on the old Jewish homily, had a tremendous appeal to the common man— "Come unto me all ye who are weak and heavy laden. . . ." It gave a dignity of life to the lowliest people. Will power to do good, application of common sense to everyday problems, and neighborliness were the keynotes of his teaching. He was a man of uncommonly open mind, as witness some of his lectures: "Render unto Caesar the things that are Caesar's, and unto God the things that are God's. . . . Let him who is without sin among you cast the first stone at her." His teaching was aimed at spiritual rather than at physical things; at character-building rather than at power or wealth; at evaluating man by what he is rather than by what he has. It was a religion which was intended to be a way of life, not a ritual shell.

It remained for Saul, a Pharisee, a Roman-Jewish tentmaker of Tarsus, to rescue Christianity from the oblivion of other Messianic cults and give it a world meaning. At first he had persecuted the Nazarenes, but later he had been converted. Through his own experience he knew that the old Judaic law was insufficient, and he came to think of Jesus as a personal *Redeemer, Saviour,* or *Lord,* through whom he and all mankind could attain personal *salvation.* These terms were all well known, meaningful terms to the mystery cults of Cybele and Mithras, and so were easily assimilated by followers of the new religion. To attract the Greek intellectuals, the idea of the Logos from Philo's philosophy was also absorbed (Philo had taught that God, the All-father, had contact with the earth and man only through an intermediary known variously as "the Logos," "the Word," "the Son of God," or "the Holy Ghost").

Jesus always remained a Jew; but Saul, the Jew, became Paul, the Christian founder. Where Jesus had been a prophet and a dreamer, Paul was a statesman, a builder, and an organizer. Paul's religion took root in Antioch, where probably the contemptuous term "Christian" was first used, but from the first it was a proselyting religion. The Christian missionaries started small Christian communities in cities where want and poverty were greatest, and from these the faith spread. Paul's letters (in Greek) to these Christian communities provide much of the material for the New Testament.

In addition to Paul's letters the most important part of the New Testament is made up of the four Gospels. Although named after four of the disciples, they were not written by them. No doubt a biography of Jesus in his own language, Aramaic, was written, and the Gospels were drawn from this, although the original is now lost. The Gospels were written in Greek a generation or two after Christ—the earliest one, Mark, about the year 65, and the latest, John, about 100.

Paul was the real founder of a Christian religion. He developed the idea of Christ as both divine and human and drew a parallel between him and the older salvation cults, introducing a new ethic in an old form. He divorced Christ from Judaism. Not averse to the acceptance of pagan rituals to spread his new religion, he admitted much that was pagan. He took over the Mithraic Sun-day rather than the Hebrew Sabbath. The Mithraic holy days, especially Christmas, Easter, and Epiphany, were adopted. The spring festival of Ostara became the Christian festival of the resurrection (Easter)—a moving anniversary of a fixed event. The twelve days from Christmas to Epiphany according to the ancients marked a means of forecasting events of the coming year— one day for each month. Mithraic sacramental ritual was preferred to Jewish temple sacrifice. Christ became the "Son of God" supernaturally conceived of the Virgin Mary, and pictures of Mary and Jesus which had a remarkable resemblance to older pictures of Horus and Osiris were set up in the churches. The mass was essentially the old sacrament of the Mithraic taurobolia. The numerous columned cathedrals were reminiscent of the groves used for worship by earlier people. As late as the Middle Ages we find gargoyles on the outside of churches exhibiting the lost condition of those outside the church while saints' images within show the benefits of salvation.

Christianity had a great advantage over other mystery religions because it offered a real human being to worship, and it had real gospels as evidence. Although it absorbed pagan forms it never became pagan in spirit, but retained its

Jewish puritanism and always avoided sensuality. As long as
it had to fight for existence it remained strong and pure, but
as soon as it had gained permanence it became softer and
weaker and schisms appeared. Each community organized
its own ecclesia with its own officers who were soon to become political as well as religious leaders.

By the end of the second century, Christianity had a
larger following than any other cult. The Roman government, usually tolerant of all religions, persecuted the Christians on three grounds. First, the Romans held them to be
unpatriotic because they foretold the fall of the Empire,
would not sacrifice to the emperor, and refused to perform
military service or accept state office. Secondly, they maintained that the Christians were antisocial because they did
not participate in festivals. Thirdly, the Romans thought
them immoral because families sometimes broke up when
some became Christianized. The second point may explain
why pagan festival days were adopted by the Christian
Church. For example, Diocletian proclaimed himself a sun-
god, and celebrated his birthday on December 25th—possibly the Christians kept this festival to all outward appear-
ances while actually worshipping Christ. Most of the persecution was sporadic, and Christianity still continued to
expand. For a time in the third century every Roman citizen
had to carry a *libellus*, a certificate showing that he had
sacrificed to the Emperor which he must exhibit on demand,
and during this period persecution was most severe because
the Christians would not conform.

By the beginning of the fourth century, emperors like
Galerius and Constantine were beginning to realize the support they might get from this sect to bolster the crumbling
Empire. In 313 the Edict of Milan was passed giving Christianity equality with emperor-worship and other religions.
Constantine made a special effort to gain Christian support—
clergy were exempted from taxes, churches were built at
government expense, the Church was granted its own courts,
Sunday was made a legal holiday. Favoring of Christianity
was continued by later emperors, until finally paganism was
suppressed in the middle of the fifth century by the The-
odosian Code, 438, and all citizens were required to be
members of the orthodox Church. The new religion spread

very rapidly among the barbarian Germanic tribes on the outskirts of the Empire, and the Holy Catholic Church— forerunner of the Holy Roman Empire—grew up quickly. As it became more powerful, heresy became punishable, even by death.

The Church was lowly in origin. With its greatest appeal to the poor and downtrodden, it grew most rapidly in the cities. Christianity stressed the importance of the future life, and thus made the burden of this life lighter for such people. This view was diametrically opposite the usual pagan Greek and Roman belief that this life was the highest attainable. The early Medieval stage in Church development is marked by numerous hermits and anchorites, by withdrawal from the world, and by asceticism or self-inflicted punishment.

Higher Greek learning and art were brought into the Church by men like Augustine, Constantine, and Gregory I. Church architecture developed the Roman basilica, with numerous columns supporting the roof, and clerestory windows. The churches became ornately decorated with mosaics, images, stained glass, and vessels of precious metals. New converts were attracted by the teaching that salvation depended on the Church (sic—not Christ), with baptism to wipe out past and original sin, and absolution to take care of relapses. The divine power of the Church was attested by the miracles of the saints. Monks began collections of manuscripts and made copies of them for other church libraries—a practice which was to preserve much Greek and Latin culture and literature through the Dark Ages. To avoid numerous interpretations and heresies in the Church, Constantine had the Nicene Creed, an official statement of belief, promulgated in 325. In part this creed states: "We believe in One God, the Father Almighty, Maker of all things . . . and in one Lord Jesus Christ, the Son of God, begotten of the Father . . . one in substance with the Father . . . who for . . . men and salvation came down and was made flesh, was made man, suffered, rose again the third day, ascended into Heaven, and cometh to judge the quick and the dead; and in the Holy Ghost. . . ." This creed, still used today in some churches, was the forerunner of the more expanded, more popular Athanasian Creed.

In the first centuries there was very little organization in the Church, because the Christians looked for the speedy 'return of Christ. Each Christian community was under the guidance of a leader known as a presbyter or priest—Greek *presbys*, "old man." Gradually as the Church expanded, church work became a full-time job and these priests became the clergy, as distinguished from the laity. The chief priest in the city became a bishop, and the bishop in the chief city of the state became an archbishop—a hierarchy similar to the political organization of the Roman Empire. Five of the chief archbishops became very influential, and took the title of "patriarch"—those at Antioch, Jerusalem, Alexandria, Constantinople, and Rome. It should be noted here that four of the patriarchates were in the East, only one in the West, and that there was only one other strong bishop in the West, at Carthage.

The Roman patriarchate gradually achieved greater and greater influence. This was due to several causes—the Roman Church was thought to have been founded by St. Peter specially commissioned by Christ (cf. Matt. 16:18–19 in the New Testament); Rome was the capital of Empire and was looked to for leadership; the early patriarchs were strong men and able statesmen who preserved order at Rome in a disintegrating empire; and Rome was the fountainhead of much missionary endeavor. Pope Leo I, 440–461, had the emperor declare the Bishop of Rome supreme head of the Christian Church in 445. The Bishop of Constantinople was set over the Eastern Church a few years later. Gregory the Great, Pope 590–604, a great writer and statesman, took over the government of Rome, which was retained by the papacy for twelve centuries. At first all Church officers of the rank of bishop or higher were called "pope," and it was not until the time of Gregory VII in the eleventh century that the title "Pope" was reserved to the Roman bishop.

One of the greatest Christian thinkers, and one very influential in spreading the power of the Bishop of Rome was Augustine (354–430), a bishop in one of the African churches. *The Confessions of St. Augustine*, one of his earliest books, is a guide to all Christians who feel themselves tempted. In his *City of God* he outlined an invisible catholic Christian state, scarcely distinguishable from the organized Church. This book ended all intellectual liberty on the part of the believer, who was admonished to submit without reservation to the Church and the Pope. The barbarians were threatened with the power of the Church over the life hereafter and became easy converts—one good result was a modification of their fierceness, and another was preservation of Greek and Roman culture throughout the Dark Ages.

Under Justinian, state support was taken from the philosophical universities and given to the Church, with the result that some magnificent buildings were constructed. Perhaps most imposing is the great Church of St. Sophia in Constantinople, built about 532–537 at a cost of eighteen tons of gold plus the work of ten thousand laborers over a period of five years. The architects abandoned the older basilica form and adopted the dome, which was to remain popular for centuries. The dome of St. Sophia's is vast—one hundred and eighty-three feet high—and is probably the most imposing interior still extant from early times. It was seized by the Turks when they took Constantinople, and has been used as a Moslem mosque since 1453. The great Christian mosaics were covered either with huge plaques or with several coats of whitewash. In recent times, permission has been granted to clean the mosaics, with a revelation of magnificent art made of fine coloring in glass and marble cubes inlaid with gold and silver.

When the Empire began to break, the Church first separated itself from secular control, and then seized temporal as well as spiritual authority. As a rich and powerful Church-state, it claimed the right to govern all true Christians. It taught that the Church was supreme rather than subject to king and emperor. The Pope was supreme judge, administrator, and lawgiver; final interpreter of Scriptures, and possessor of the keys of Heaven itself. His legate took precedence over all the Church hierarchy. All except the Jews were under the jurisdiction of the Church. The Church levied taxes and administered justice, using excommunication as its most potent penalty for violations. A whole new code of "canon law" was developed, and some of the clergy devoted themselves to this branch of Church work. Canon law was applied to all trials of the clergy and to all offenses against the Church such as heresy, atheism, adultery, and sacrilege. Immense revenues accrued from Church property and collection of the tithe, in addition to rich bequests. The Church became the center of social life. It directed all education, dispensed all charity, controlled all the universities and book publishers, and conducted all hospitals. All matters pertaining to family life—marriage, divorce, birth and death records, succession, and wills—were in its hands. The Church couriers acted as a means of communication and as censors, the clergy considering themselves agents of God to guide man's thoughts and actions. The Church maintained the idea that it controlled the entrance to Heaven, thus emphasizing the importance of a threat of excommunication which would act as a bar to Heaven's gates. Some evils crept in, as we shall see, notably patronage and appointments to Church offices made by laymen, which resulted in many of the lower clergy being illiterate and worldly men.

As the Church advanced in power and importance, so the sacramental rituals increased in number, variety, and elaboration. A sacrament was defined as a sign of inward grace and required three things: matter, or the physical element; form, or the specified ritual; and intention, or ministration by a competent person. In the Dark Ages the sacraments were often treated as a fetish, and were used to effect "faith cures" or to ward off evil. Eventually the number of sacraments recognized by the Church was reduced to seven:

1. Baptism of the newborn child, to take away original sin and give the child a modicum of free will or ability to do good.

2. Confirmation, or laying on of hands, at adolescence, to claim the individual for God.

3. The Eucharist, or sacrament of the Lord's Supper. At first the communicant took only the wafer, the priest both wine and wafer. Mass was always characterized by the miracle of transubstantiation and was accompanied by elaborate ritual, lights, incense, and rich vessels.

4. Confession, followed by penance. At first this was voluntary, but after the opening of the thirteenth century (from 1215) it was required at least once a year.

5. Extreme unction, just before death, the anointing with oil of the sense organs, loins, and feet.

6. Holy orders, performed for each priest by the bishop.

7. Marriage, which made the union of man and woman and childbearing legitimate for the laity.

Chapter XIII

Orthodoxy versus Heresy

THE church organization early became extensive. We have already seen how, from a group of itinerant preachers, the hierarchy of the church was built up with priest, bishop, archbishop, and patriarch. At the same time bureaucracy extended downward. The advantages of belonging to the church organization were many, and we find deacons to supervise charity, exorcists to attend the mentally deranged and the sick, janitors to tend the church property, subdeacons to assist the deacons, acolytes to assist the bishops, lectors to read the Scriptures and assist the priest, and so on ad infinitum.

Some few men, however, should be largely credited with shaping the Church. We have already seen the work of Gregory and Innocent III. Another important "father" was Augustine, 354-430. He believed that with the fall of Adam all men fell, but that some were redeemed by the grace of God. There was no place for "free will" in his belief, but simple predestination determined who should be saved. He held that the Church was based on apostolicity, unity, universality, and holiness; that it was the supreme authority in intellectual, spiritual, temporal, and moral realms. He identified the Church with the Kingdom of God, and promulgated the theory that only through it and its sacraments could one attain salvation. The later Church challenged his theory of predestination, and proposed that Divine grace bestowed at baptism wiped out original sin and gave man a measure of free will, thus making him responsible for his works and actions.

Another pillar of orthodox belief was Athanasius. He was recognized as the chief proponent of the Logos doctrine, that is the doctrine that Christ and God were one and the same in substance and attributes. His definition of Christianity was faith in redemption through the God-man Christ. At the Council of Nicaea in 325 his view was adopted as correct and formed the basis of the Nicene Creed.

As the Church increased in size and advanced toward universality in Europe, many shortcomings appeared. The papal rule of temporal leaders provoked much conflict as we have seen. Attempts to increase Church revenue sometimes caused serious hardship, aggravated by greedy bishops with plural benefices, absentee clergy, and low-paid vicars. Priests who kept mistresses were often favored by the populace in spite of the bad moral example, because the girls of the community would be less liable to unwelcome advances. An illiterate priesthood which exploited the populace by charging fees for administration of sacraments added to the evils in the Church and detracted from its prestige. The common people continued to mix much superstition, divination, and even sorcery with their religion. Many doubted, and lived in worldly ways in spite of the threat of excommunication. Fostered by lack of good religious instruction, it is small surprise that many heresies arose.

One of the earliest of these came out of the East. It was Arianism, a pure monotheistic belief which proposed that God alone was God. The Arians denied the divinity of Christ, claiming that he was human only. The controversy over this heresy resulted in the first ecumenical Church conference at Nicaea in 325. Athanasius opposed Arius and was successful in having Arianism voted in error by the conference. To fortify his position, the Nicene, or Athanasian, Creed, was formulated. Fourteen of the seventeen bishops in Arius' following recanted, but Arianism did not disappear until about the eighth century.

A more widespread heretical group were the Gnostics, who believed in two deities, a Supreme Being and a lesser spirit of evil. They flatly denied the human body of Christ, and proclaimed him a phantom spirit who came from the Supreme Being to give enlightenment and knowledge to mankind. Very early to combat this heresy the Apostle's Creed was promulgated—note that this creed is not a statement of fundamental Christianity, but is aimed against the belief of the Gnostics. To bolster the orthodox faith a body of Scripture was compiled, which became the New Testament. When the Gnostics declared that they could find their teaching in allegory in the New Testament, the claim that the "Church" was the only body that could interpret the Scripture was put forth. This was a new expression at that time, but was to spread in current use until the Church had a monopoly of both truth and salvation. Another means of combatting heresy appeared when some bishops began to claim "Apostolic succession" to their seats, that is, began to assert that they had received their authority directly from the Apostles with special directions and interpretations to be passed on only to their successors.

A heresy that caused great concern in the eleventh and twelfth centuries was Catharism (promulgated by the Cathari, or Albigenses) which was an outgrowth of Gnosticism entering Western Europe through Bulgaria. The Cathari believed in the dualism of God, that there was a universe of two principles, either spirit and matter or good and evil. Their God of Evil was identified with Jehovah of the Old Testament, connected with pestilence, war, and matter, whereas their God of Good was revealed in the New Testament as entirely beneficent and connected with brotherly love, charity, and the spirit. They declared that tales of the virgin birth, crucifixion, and resurrection were impossibilities because Christ was purely spirit. They preached that His life was exemplary, not expiatory. They believed in the transmigration of souls, and that all would eventually attain salvation, either after this life or after reincarnation. They abolished such refinements or elaborations as the use of incense, use of the cross, veneration of saints and images, baptism of infants, the Mass, and the doctrine of transubstantiation.

All the Cathari were divided into two classes—the perfect and the believers. Any believer could become perfect by laying on of hands and by swearing to refrain from money-making, shedding of blood, and use of profanity; to abstain from flesh, milk, cheese, and eggs; and to live henceforth a celibate life. Very few Cathari were "perfect," but from these were chosen the clergy both for regular work and for missionary endeavor. Every believer was required to become perfected at least at the hour of death. Suicide was permissible after the perfecting ceremony (the Consolamentum).

Catharism was popular because of its high ethical teachings, because of its attacks on the wealth of the Church, and because of its diatribes against the immorality of the clergy. By the end of the twelfth century the Church was so concerned that it called on the various European rulers to stamp out this heresy. The attempt met with so little success that in 1209 the Pope declared a Crusade against the Albigenses. Like persecution in many places in history, this did not extinguish the heresy, but succeeded only in driving the movement underground.

Still another important heretical group were the Waldensians, who wished not to break away from the Church but rather to reform it by a return to poverty and simplicity. Peter Waldo founded this group in 1170 in Lyons. He personally fell under canon law as an unlicensed preacher and was excommunicated, but his movement spread. His followers adopted a simple dark religious habit and sandals. Their teaching was based entirely on the four Gospels, which they believed were just as meaningful in the vernacular as in the Latin. They recognized the Scriptures rather than the Pope as the final authority, refusing to admit the papal authority or the powers of binding and loosing claimed to be possessed by the Church. Neither did they admit that the Pope possessed the keys of Heaven. They held that merit rather than ordination gave effective value to the sacraments. They developed a Waldensian Church with their own clergy, who took vows of poverty and chastity and led pure lives. Their church simplified the old ritual, and rejected three institutions of the Roman Church—purgatory, Mass for the dead, and invocation of saints. This sect made considerable headway, especially among the lower classes.

To combat heresy, the Church instituted the Inquisition for its detection and suppression. The Inquisition was a gradual growth from the eleventh century on, but was well established and almost entirely under direction of the Dominicans (see Chapter XV) by the middle of the thirteenth century. The prime object of the Inquisition was to gain a confession, for only in this way could the soul of the heretic be redeemed. The usual procedure was to preach a sermon on the orthodox faith and then ask all heretics to confess. The next step was to ask the faithful and the recent confessors to report any heretics they knew. After being reported, there was only one way for a proclaimed heretic to establish his innocence and gain freedom. The accused named all his personal enemies, and if the accuser's name was on the list he was then freed. Otherwise, there was never an acquittal, and a confession was extorted. Kindness and persuasion were first used, then curtailment of diet, then prevention of sleep and threat of torture, and finally actual torture on the rack or strappado. The rack was an instrument on which the victim was tied hand and foot. Then by means of a windlass the unfortunate fellow was stretched until he either gave in or had his joints dislocated. On the strappado the martyr was suspended by the wrists, raised to the ceiling, and dropped to within a few inches of the floor—a performance repeated until the sufferer submitted. In some countries other refined methods of torture were used—the boot, the thumbscrew, or the iron maiden. All penalties were expiatory, and might take the form of imprisonment, forced attendance at Mass a certain number of times, a pilgrimage, a Crusade, or the public wearing of a yellow cross for a fixed period. Relapsed heretics were inexpiable, and were handed over to the state for execution, later (in the fourteenth century) to burning at the stake. Probably the number of executions, while large, is grossly exaggerated, as it is unlikely that more than 10 per cent of heretics were convicted. It is generally conceded that the Franciscans and Dominicans did far more to control heresy by preaching and teaching than was done by either Crusades or the Inquisition.

By the end of the fourteenth century, the Church was due for a transition. Protestantism was soon to make its advent. We should note here, therefore, five points that distinguish the Medieval Church from the Modern Church. First, the Medieval Church required compulsory membership. Secondly, its revenue was derived not only from voluntary contributions but also from fees, tithes, and Church property. Thirdly, the Church was a single unified body. Fourthly, the Pope could relax human laws by granting a special dispensation. Lastly, the Medieval Church exercised many functions now relegated to the state, controlling such matters as courts, canon law, usury, sorcery, prisons, marriage, and wills. By the end of the sixteenth century every one of these principles was to be abandoned.

Chapter XIV

History of the Papacy

THE power of the patriarch at Rome continued in the ascendant. The Roman Church was wealthy and strong, with no rival in the West, and, in addition to certain inherent advantages mentioned previously, had imperious patriarchs like Stephen, Clement, Siricius, and Victor who acted with high-handed authority to gain their ends. The Bishop of Rome was finally granted legal power as a judge of appeal for all Christian churches by the Council of Sardica (now Sophia) about 344. Because this council was not a ecumenical (i.e., a universal church) council, the decree was not recognized as valid; and perhaps more influential was the encouragement by Innocent I, 402–417, of sending problems to Rome. The first real Pope, or Primate of the Christian Church, was Leo I, 440–461, the strong man of Italy in his time.

By the fifth century the practice of veneration of saints as intermediaries was becoming common in the Christian Church. Each saint had a special function and specially reserved holy days—they filled the role of the lesser deities in the old pagan religions. Relics of bones and clothing were thought to possess miraculous powers. The result was the widespread practice of pilgrimage to tombs and the trade (not always honest) in relics. The practice of pilgrimage led centuries later to the Crusades to the Holy Land.

Gregory I was destined to become greater than any of his predecessors. He was from a wealthy aristocratic family, received a good education, had close contact with the rigors of monastic life, and had established several monasteries before his election to the papacy in 590. During the fourteen years of his ministry he established firmly the temporal authority of the Pope in and around Rome. A good administrator of the papal estates, he did much to alleviate poverty and correct abuses in management. The first monk to become a Pope, he used his authority with the regular clergy to spread the influence of the See of Rome. Through the establishment of courts and missions he was able to do much to centralize authority and unify the Western Church. Many popular ideas in Church theology were his. He developed the ideas of penance and purgatory. He taught that for every sin there must be an atonement by good works. If the sins outweighed the good works, the righteous could still gain Heaven by suffering for a period in purgatory, but for the unrighteous there was no salvation. Purgatorial suffering could be relieved by celebration of the Mass and by the prayers of the righteous still living on the earth.

The next two centuries saw great increase in the wealth of the Church. Through gifts made in return for prayer and Mass after death, the Church by 800 A.D. was the greatest single landowner in Europe. At that time it was said that the Church owned one-third of France and similar huge holdings in other countries. The year 800 marked a further step in increased power of the Pope. Pepin drove the Lombards out of central Italy and gave their lands as a personal gift to the Pope, thus making him a landed prince. In return, the Pope crowned Pepin's son, Charlemagne, as Emperor of the Romans, marking the beginning of two things familiar to the Middle Ages—the Holy Roman Empire and coronation of emperors by the Pope.

The middle of the ninth century saw further great advance in papal power. Nicholas I, Pope from 858 to 867, established control of the national clergy, and succeeded in gaining some measure of authority over certain acts of rulers. Through the so-called "False Decretals" the authority of the Pope was greatly enhanced and extended and temporal authority over him was greatly reduced.

The darkest period of papal history began just at the end of the ninth century and lasted for sixty-seven years. Twenty Popes succeeded each other in what became generally known as the "Rule of the Harlots." The Lateran Palace became a resort of orgies and degradation. The mistresses of the "celibate" Popes made their sons successors to the papacy. Murder, assassination, fighting, prostitution, and bribery were the order of the day.

An end to this immorality, debauchery, and infamy came in 962–963 when Otto the German cleared out the remnants of this papal line, set up a new Pope, and took for himself and his successors the right of papal nomination—a great blow to the prestige and authority of the Pope. Otto also seized the chance to make appointments of the higher clergy. As he needed to bolster the Empire it was more vital to him to have good statesmen than good churchmen, and this again weakened the Church power, by increasing the evil known as lay-investiture, or choice of churchmen by laymen.

By the year 1000 there were four chief evils to be found in the Church. Much land owned by the Church was still held under the feudal organization, and bishops and abbots had to pay homage to a temporal lord as well as to the Pope. It was to the advantage of the overlord to get men in these positions who were loyal to him, and this led to lay-investiture, or appointment of bishops contrary to canon law. Because of the wealth and influence of the Church, positions in connection with it were greatly coveted: and where princes controlled appointments, purchase of position, or simony, was a common practice. To get their outlay back, the higher clergy after buying a benefice from a prince, sold the lesser posts to the lower clergy—often to the highest bidder rather than to the best qualified man. Marriage of the clergy, though forbidden, had crept in, especially in Germany, and was the third evil because it tended to disperse Church property and to divide the interest of the priest. A fourth evil was the part played by the people in election of the Pope. The Popes of the eleventh century fought against these evils, ably advised by men like Damiani, Humbert, and Hildebrand. The Cluny reforms of this century tried to overcome three of these evils by removing from office all those convicted of simony, by enforcing the law of celibacy of the clergy, and by placing the appointment of the Pope in the hands of the College of Cardinals, a small body of high advisers to the Pope (the system still used today in the Roman Catholic Church).

The first election of the College of Cardinals resulted in the appointment of Hildebrand as Pope Gregory VII. Gregory made his program reform of the Church, separation of Church and state, and supremacy of the papacy over both

Church and state. He claimed unlimited authority over the clergy as supreme and universal bishop. There was no appeal from papal decree, and the papal legate took precedence over all other clergy. He claimed that the Pope was also supreme temporal leader. His sanction was required on all writings and interpretations. In a synod at Rome in 1074 he denounced simony and reenacted the laws requiring celibacy of the clergy. There was a great deal of opposition to this ruling, especially in Germany, the lower clergy being especially desirous of leading a normal family life. In 1075 he condemned lay-investiture, but the struggle over this point was to continue for another half-century, and sporadically for even longer.

At Sutri in 1111 Pope Paschal II made the suggestion that he would relinquish all feudal claims and rely for income on gifts and tithes if, in return, the emperor would give up his right of investiture. There was considerable opposition to the suggestion, but an agreement was finally reached by the Concordat of Worms, 1122. By this agreement, the Church gained the right of appointment of bishops and of investiture with ring and staff—the secular symbols of authority. The emperor was permitted to be present at the ceremony, was allowed to veto the appointment of anyone unfriendly to himself, and had the right of appointment in case of dispute. After the religious investiture, the emperor granted temporal power by presentation of the scepter to the new bishop. This was really a compromise arrangement, but the Church had made clear its position that the bishop was first of all a part of a religious organization and only secondly a feudal lord. Except for some trouble with Frederick Barbarossa in the late twelfth century, the Concordat of Worms settled the investiture problem.

The papacy attained the climax of its power at the opening of the thirteenth century during the time of Pope Innocent III, 1198–1216. An ascetic young man—only thirty-seven when he became Pope—Innocent showed his contempt for the world by domination of it. He claimed to be not only a priest but also a feudal overlord of the whole Christian world. In politics he was a realist, expediency rather than ethics being his guiding policy. Every opportunity was seized to spread his temporal authority. The first step

was establishment of power in the "Papal States," free from
authority of the Holy Roman Emperor. The marital difficul-
ties of King Philip Augustus gave him the necessary excuse
for interference in France. In England he was able to make
King John bow before him and to accept Stephen Langton
as Archbishop of Canterbury—even forcing John to hand
over his crown and receive back his realm as a fief. In the
Empire he played the House of Brunswick against the House
of Hohenstaufen so effectively that the latter became extinct.
In return for the Pope's support, Frederick II promised a
Crusade, which resulted in the cession of Jerusalem, Nazareth, and Bethlehem. In 1215 he called a great congress at
the Lateran Palace, which became the most magnificent
spectacle to its time. The pomp and splendor was enhanced
by the fact that nearly every great prince in Christendom was
in attendance. It is said that the gifts of gold and jewels
were so great that a whole army of servants was kept busy
storing them away.

Probably the great Lateran meeting marked the zenith
of papal influence. The Church had established its claim
that the Pope was the final ultimate earthly authority and
that its own purpose was to guide men spiritually and morally to show them the way of salvation. Now a decline was
to set in, to which many factors contributed. It should be
noted at this point that a double hierarchy had grown up in
the Church with the Pope at the head of both groups—the
secular clergy, made up of archbishop, bishop, and priest;
and the regular clergy, made up of heads of orders, abbots,
and monks. The regular orders, especially the Franciscans and
Dominicans, were widespread, and did a great deal of good
work in education, culture, and charity, as well as in the
spreading of good cheer.

It would be hard to overestimate the importance of the
Church at about 1200. It kept touch with its people from the
cradle to the grave through the various sacraments. These
sacraments gave even the lowliest man a feeling of importance. Together with elaborate ritual and rich ceremonial,
they provided a bright spot in the otherwise drab existence
of the lower classes—taking the place of modern entertainment such as radio and cinema. The numerous holy days
(holi-days) eased the life of the working classes also. The

finest work of artisan and artist was encouraged by the Church for the Church—architectural design, sculpture, stained glass, paintings, vessels, vestments, and ornaments. In the economic sphere it stood for a just price, fair wages, and no interest. Church courts were developed to deal with the clergy, marriage, divorce, and inheritance. The Church controlled all communication lines of the times and thus had a hand in all international diplomatic relations. It tried to maintain peace, or at least to reduce conflict, by declaring the "Truce of God," which forbade fighting between Wednesday night and Monday morning, forbade fighting on holy days, and made the conferring of knighthood a religious ceremony. Many court counsellors were taken from the educated clergy, both regular and secular. The aim of the Church seems to have been a way of life applicable in everyday affairs.

Some evils and weaknesses were bound to appear. Unworthy leaders brought loss of prestige. The Church was built up in an economy of poverty, and found adjustment to new conditions of wealth and power difficult. The Crusades, beneficial though they were, contributed to the weakening of the Church. They strengthened the position of the kings by bleeding away the nobles. The stimulus to business resulted in a middle class opposed to the rigorous control of the Church in business and finance. The broadening of men's minds and the spread of learning weakened the Church, because men began to think for themselves. Independent thought led to tension inside, to unorthodox beliefs, and eventually to schisms. Science is always opposed to authority, and every advance weakened the position of the Pope.

Near the end of the thirteenth century, Pope Boniface undid much of the good work of Innocent III and contributed to the weakening of the papacy. When he forbade the clergy to pay taxes, Philip of France retaliated by putting an embargo on the export of money and jewels from France, and Edward I of England seized the temporal holdings of some benefices in lieu of taxes. Thus did Boniface lose not only revenue but prestige. A more far-reaching result, and in the long run a harder blow to the papacy, was the election in 1305 of a French archbishop as Pope, who chose to set up his seat at Avignon in France rather than at Rome. From 1305 to 1377 we find a line of Avignon Popes—a period often referred to in Church history as the "Baby-lonian Captivity" of the Church. Two outstanding results of the Avignon papacy were the extermination of the Order of Knights Templars at the instigation of the French king, who wanted their property, and the introduction of new ways to increase the papal revenue, made necessary because many would not recognize the Avignon Popes. The second of the French Popes, Pope John XXII, introduced seven new sources of revenue: the annates, usually half of the first year's revenue in a new benefice, originally an emergency measure but now made permanent; the spolia, a right of seizure of the movable property of deceased bishops, originally be-longing to his relatives; the tithe, a 10 per cent tax made universal on all incomes except those of cardinals and Knights of St. John; revenues from vacant benefices; visitation fees; proceeds from the sale of indulgences; fees for legal settle-ments or for special dispensations. A third result, of lesser importance, was the great impetus given to Avignon—bank-ers, merchants, usurers, prostitutes, artisans, and others flocked to the city to gain a portion of the new wealth.

Several attempts were made to move the papal seat back to Rome, but the French Popes were unwilling to sacrifice French luxury for Roman austerity. In 1378 the Great West-ern Schism occurred, following which there were two Popes for several years—one at Avignon, one at Rome. This resulted in endless confusion, loss of prestige, a general falling away from the Church, and the rise of new heresies (notably the Lollard followers of John Wycliffe and John Hus). In 1409, the papacy lost more prestige when the Council of Pisa agreed that an ecumenical council rather than the Pope was the supreme authority in the Church. The council then pro-ceeded to depose both Popes and elected a new one, but as neither of the old Popes would recognize his deposition this only increased the confusion by the addition of a third Pope. A second council was called at Constance in 1414 to heal the Schism, to extirpate heresy, and to reform the Church. This council was successful in deposing the Popes, but then argued whether a new election or reform should take pre-cedence. Finally a new Pope was elected, but practically no reforms resulted. John Hus had been given a safe-conduct to this council to defend himself against a charge of heresy, but the safe-conduct was ignored and he was burned—this was the sole attempt to fulfill the second object of the council. It was further decided that each nation should settle its own problems with the Pope by concordat. An attempt to make the ecumenical council a permanent arrangement to meet at certain fixed times proved abortive.

Chapter XV

Monasteries and Missionaries

MONASTICISM

MONASTICISM arose very early in the Christian community. A result of early Christian asceticism and puritanism, it first appeared as an anchorite movement. The hermits and anchorites were first found in Egypt, and were similar to the hermits of the Eastern religions, with self-inflicted maceration of the body and self-renunciation a definite part of their life. The idea of communal living developed much later, originally a lay movement but eventually adopted by the Church. Probably the system was transplanted to Europe by Athanasius, but many bishops contributed to the organization as it was finally constituted. Basil of Caesarea gave the three original vows of chastity, poverty, and obedience. Under the four great "Doctors" of the Western Church—Jerome, Augustine, Ambrose of Milan, and Gregory—the monastic movement spread very rapidly, and during the fifth century came to include women. John Cassian early in the fifth century established two monasteries at Marseilles —St. Victor and St. Mary—one for men, one for women. His two treatises for their guidance, the *Institutes* and the *Conferences*, contributed much to the way of life in monasteries in general.

Benedict of Nursia, 480–543, was the greatest organizer, and under the name of St. Benedict is the best known of the early monks. He drew up a *Rule*, or constitution, for the conduct of monks and monasteries (hence the name "regular clergy," from the Latin *regula*, rule). The Benedictine *Rule* set forth a sane, comprehensible, temperate asceticism with explicit instruction for each part of the day. Recognizing that all were not fitted for monastic life, Benedict initiated a probationary period, or novitiate, of one year before one was

permitted to take the monastic vows. Democracy was in-
stanced in the election of the abbot by the monks, but after
his election every monk was required to take a vow of obedience to him. The vow of poverty was very stringent, articles
of everyday personal use and even clothing belonging to
the monastery. The vow of celibacy was also required and
strictly enforced, because marriage would have made conventual life impossible. Frequent prayer and meditation
were required. There were seven regular daily periods of devotion, lasting about twenty minutes each. These were
"nocturn" at midnight, "prime" at six in the morning,
"tierce" at nine, "sext" at twelve, "none" (our noon) at
three, "vespers" at sundown, and "compline" on retiring.
Undue fasting was discouraged, and two nourishing meals
were served daily, one after sext and the other after vespers.
The monks were encouraged to lead a normal healthy life,
and self-inflicted punishment was deprecated. Constant occupation was considered desirable, and so they were required to
raise the necessary crops for support of the abbey, to cook
their own meals, to do their own laundry, to read, to teach,
and to copy books and manuscripts.

The monasteries themselves followed a regular plan. The
conventual church was built in the form of a cross with the
top (or front) toward the east, and here was placed the
altar. Outside, usually bordering the south wall of the church
was the "cloister," or covered walk, built around an open
quadrangle. In the cloister, usually facing south for good
light, was the library or "scriptorium," and here most copy-
ing of manuscripts was done. On the west side was the school-
room, and on one of the other two sides the "lavatory" or
washroom. Opening off the cloister on the outside were the
"dorter" or dormitory (close to the church to facilitate the
nocturn devotion), the chapter house, the warming house,
the "frater" or refectory (dining room), the kitchen, and the
"cellarium" or supply house. In a separate residence lived the
abbot. At a little distance, for the sake of quiet, was the infirmary for the sick and the aged with its own kitchen. Sur-
rounding the buildings were the gardens, orchards, fields, fish
pond, and mill of the monastery.

A great portion of the monk's time was spent in the cloister,
for here he did his writing, reading, studying, and teaching.

All monks slept in the common dormitory. Only in the warming house was a fire permitted, and here also the rule of silence or solemnity was relaxed. In the refectory the two meals were served. Strict silence was enjoined at mealtime except that one of the monks read aloud the Scripture while the others ate. The cellarium was under the jurisdiction of the cellarer, who had charge of the business transactions of the abbey. The second floor of the cellarium served as a guesthouse, or hotel, for middle-class travellers—upper-class guests stayed in the abbot's house, while the lower classes were kept in the almony near the gate. A guest was allowed free lodging for two days and nights, and was usually accommodated longer if ill. Each monk spent three days every two months in the infirmary to be bled, and welcomed this as a holiday because of the relaxation afforded and also because infirmary food was more choice and provided a change from the food from the refectory kitchen.

Early monks like St. Augustine and St. Boniface were often zealous, hard-working pioneers, but with wealth came decay and departure from the Benedictine Rule. Some attempts at reform were made, and one or two revivals are notable. At Cluny a return to the earlier ideals was sought, with recognition of supremacy of the Pope a keynote. The return to agricultural pursuits was successful for a time, and many followers were gathered; but with fame came wealth and the inevitable decay. The abbey church at Cluny was the greatest architectural achievement in church building before the erection of St. Paul's in Rome. Many reformers emphasized the hermit ideal, and this movement was popular for a time. Another group were the Cistercians, who established their abbey at Citeaux in 1098. They returned to primitive simplicity in religion, and are noted for their monastic puritanism. Their robes were white because any dye would have been a refinement, and they permitted the use of no gold crosses, no carvings, no paintings, no stained glass, or any other elaboration. They attracted many lay brothers, and are famous for their advances in horticulture and viticulture.

The contribution of the monasteries to medieval and modern times is enormous. The most recognized contribution is the preservation of books and manuscripts and numerous translations of them during the Dark Ages. Jerome, as a monk, gave the Vulgate version of the Bible still used in the Roman Catholic Church. The roster of their great men is numberless. In addition to twenty-four Popes, the monasteries produced some famous historians, theologians statesmen, philosophers, artists, poets, and scientists—such men as Martin Luther, Erasmus, Roger Bacon, Thomas Aquinas, the Venerable Bede, Gregory, and Boniface, to mention only a few. Indirectly, as the only schools of the times, they should be credited with every advance where learning played a part. They provided sanctuary and a quiet refuge for the sick, the maimed, the scholarly, the disgraced, the friendless, and the indolent. They set good examples for the common man in agricultural and horticultural research. They were the only hospitals and inns of the day. Not least important was their missionary endeavor—their aim being not only conversion to Christianity, but subjection to Papal sovereignty.

THE MISSIONARY EFFORT

The missionary effort was not for long confined to the monks, although the churches did not organize missions until the seventeenth century. As early as the thirteenth, however, there were two orders of friars recognized by the Pope.

St. Francis of Assisi, 1181–1226, was the son of a merchant and lived a fast life in his youth. Once he narrowly escaped death, and this escape made him introspective, finally leading him to become a hermit. In 1208 he had a revelation to go out and preach, whereupon he gathered a small following and preached love of God, repentance, and assistance to the weak, the sick, and the poor. His followers had a simple rule prescribing poverty. In 1210 his following was recognized by the Pope under the official designation of "Friars Minor," better known as the Franciscans. They gave a lay interpretation of Christianity, and attracted especially the lower classes.

St. Dominic, 1170–1221, was a Spanish theologian, so appalled by the heresy he could see about him that he adopted a life of poverty and simplicity and set himself the task of winning back heretics by confidence. He and his followers were formally recognized by the Pope in 1215, under the name of "Preaching Friars," usually called Dominicans. St. Dominic himself was a scholar, and his appeal was mainly to the higher classes by logic and theology.

Both orders spread rapidly and quickly became wealthy, amassing much conventual property through gifts and bequests. Wealth brought a softening of their zeal, and decay set in. The friars differed from the monks because they were free to move about from place to place, being bound only to the order and not to a particular monastery. Both the regular and secular clergy accused them of interference in parish affairs. The Dominicans, the great scholars of the day, met the further criticism that they tended to restrict free thought. Later, as we have seen, they had almost complete control of the Inquisition for the control of heresy.

A third great missionary order was formed early in the sixteenth century. Ignatius Loyola, 1491–1556, was a noble by birth, a native of the Basque country in Spain. He served as an army officer at the court of Ferdinand and Isabella. He was wounded in the king's service in 1521, and a long illness following his wound led to his conversion to a life of piety and sacrifice. During a period of ascetic living he reported that he saw visions, and also wrote a book, *Spiritual Exercises*, which is his most widely read work. While making a pilgrimage to Jerusalem he realized his lack of knowledge and resolved to improve his education. To this end, he attended the University of Paris, 1528–1535. While there he met Francis Xavier. In 1534 these two and six others formulated the principles of the Order of the Society of Jesus, or Jesuits. They set down a rule emphasizing discipline along military lines for teachers, preachers, and confessors. The membership rapidly increased, and the new order was recognized by the Pope in 1540. Their intention had been a program of conversion and assistance in the Holy Land, but the Pope diverted their efforts to the Protestant world. Loyola became the first general of the Order and, much against his will, spent the balance of his life in Rome attending to correspondence and organization. Xavier and Spanish missionaries from Manila succeeded in converting fifty thousand Japanese before the Japanese government took a hand, forbidding its nationals to become Christianized and closing its doors to all Europeans. The Order performed great missionary endeavors in Europe, Asia, and America, but eventually degenerated and was abolished in 1773. The Pope restored it in 1814, and today it is a flourishing Roman Catholic mission effort.

The Russians were converted to Christianity by missionaries from Constantinople in the seventh and eighth centuries. When Constantinople fell to the Turks, the Tsars felt themselves divinely appointed successors to the patriarchate, and undertook to defend all true Christians who accepted the Greek Orthodox faith. Peter the Great brought the Church completely under governmental control. When the Porte granted Russia the right to protect the sultan's Christian subjects, Russia seized the excuse to expand toward the southeast. Thus did Russia set the pattern for imperialism to follow in the wake of the missions.

Missionaries—Franciscans, Dominicans, Jesuits, and others —following the New Testament injunction, "Go ye into all the world and preach the gospel to every creature," followed in the path of the explorers. Their work was manifold. They carried with them not only the Christian religion but also modern science and invention, European culture and medical knowledge. They introduced the alphabet to many peoples and reduced numerous languages to writing. They educated millions and thus conquered superstition. Their teaching did much to abolish human sacrifice and cannibalism, and in many places improved the status of womankind. Their reports on languages and customs are a gold mine for the modern historian, and their maps and charts of exploration helped open many areas to the European. Natives were encouraged to visit Europe. A demand for Western goods was created, thus opening new markets for trade. Because of their attacks on ancient tradition, they were often treated badly by native peoples, underwent severe hardships, and sometimes met death as martyrs. This gave an excuse to their governments to annex territory and establish protectorates over vast areas—a motive for imperialism.

From the seventeenth century on, we find the various churches organizing missions. Dutch and English Protestant missions were established in the East Indies in 1602. In 1622 a Roman Catholic Missionary Board was established to train missionaries for the work and to teach languages. In 1695 the Church of England formed the Society for the Promotion of Christian Knowledge. During the eighteenth century the Baptists and the Methodists established mission fields. The American Board of Foreign Missions was organized in the United States in 1810. In the last century and a half numerous Bible Societies have sprung up to translate and distribute the Scriptures in many languages. Today we accept missionary endeavor as an integral part of religious work.

Chapter XVI

The Crusades

THE most marked religious endeavor in the late eleventh century and through the twelfth and thirteenth was the Crusading movement. By the eleventh century Jerusalem had become the Holy City of the Christian world, with numerous churches, monasteries, and hospices. A steady stream of pilgrims passed in and out of the city, visiting the holy places, seeking a second baptism in the waters of the Jordan, and searching for relics. Except for payment of taxes, they had free access to the recognized shrines until the whole area was taken by the Seljuk Turks. The Byzantine emperor, Alexius, appealed to Pope Urban II for aid, and this appeal led to the First Crusade ("War of the Cross") against the Seljuks.

The Crusades were made possible by the unification at this time of Europe into three main groups—England, France, and the Holy Roman Empire. Recruiting for the early Crusades was an easy matter. Motives included devotion to the Church, desire for adventure, and avarice for the material profit that might accrue. The Crusaders escaped the feudal restrictions at home; they were freed from the interest on their debts; they were forgiven tithes and taxes. The Church ruled that a Crusade would serve as penance for all sin, and thus absolved the Crusader and practically assured him of Heaven. As a further inducement, the Church promised to care for his wife and family during his absence and in case of nonreturn.

Three knightly Crusading orders made their appearance. The earliest of these was the Knights Hospitalers, or Knights of St. John, organized for care of the sick and for charitable purposes but becoming a military order in 1113. Its members could be recognized by their habit of solid black with a white cross on breast and back. This order is still in existence, now known as the Knights of Malta. The second order was that of the Knights Templars, formed in 1118 along military lines with the monastic vows of chastity, poverty, and obedience. They served as escorts for pilgrims, becoming generally known as Red Cross Knights from their habit of white with a red cross on front and back. They were abolished by the Avignon Popes as we have already seen. A third, and lesser, order was the Teutonic Knights, formed for hospital service in 1190 but later becoming a military order. Its dress was white with a black cross. The members of these orders enjoyed even greater privileges than the ordinary Crusader. They were exempt from tax and tithe, had the right of asylum at home, were released from feudal obligations, and could not be excommunicated except by special command of the Pope.

Pope Urban II called the First Crusade at Clermont in 1095. In the following year four armies totalling over one hundred thousand men converged on Constantinople. The ranks were decimated by lack of supplies, especially water, as they crossed Asia Minor, but they succeeded in capturing Antioch in 1098 and Jerusalem in the following year—to be held for nearly a century until Saladin finally regained it in 1187. Jerusalem was made the head of a feudal organization rather than of a Church-state as the Pope had hoped. Dominated by the French, a code of laws known as the *Assizes of Jerusalem* put the same requirements and limitations on merchants and pilgrims as did the feudal system and guilds at home. Many of the Crusaders became local feudal barons, put away their European background, took Saracen brides, and adopted Oriental modes of life.

A Second Crusade, against Edessa, started in 1146 but met disaster and perished in Asia Minor. After Saladin retook Jerusalem in 1187, the Third Crusade was organized in 1189 with Emperor Frederick Barbarossa, King Richard I (Richard Cœur de Lion) of England, and King Philip Augustus of France as leaders. The Emperor was drowned while fording a river, and most of the Germans then turned back. With no third party to settle disputes, quarrels between the two kings became more violent, but they continued together until the fall of Acre, when Philip Augustus returned home with his followers. Richard continued until 1191, when he made a treaty with Saladin which gave the Christians right of access to the Holy Sepulcher in Jerusalem.

The First and Third were the two great Crusades, but the spirit that prompted them remained alive for many years. A Fourth Crusade organized by Pope Innocent III in 1202 never reached its objective because of the mixed motives and cupidity of the leaders. The Fifth was the famous Children's Crusade of 1212, which showed great fervor and devotion but resulted only in the death and slavery of the participants. The Sixth, Seventh, and Eighth Crusades were organized with various success in 1227, 1249, and 1270 respectively. The Christians were finally expelled from the Holy Land in 1291, and this defeat ended the Crusading period.

The results of the Crusades were widespread and far-reaching. The advance of the Turk was stayed. The papacy both gained and lost—lost in power as we have already noted in a previous chapter, but gained in prestige and wealth through missions in the East. The commercial revival, especially in luxury goods, was greatly accelerated. Italian cities like Venice boomed by reason of entrepôt trade from East to West. Luxuries, such as olives, silks, cottons, grapes, figs, oranges, dates, spices, lemons, cosmetics, mirrors, salt, soap, mosaics, tapestry, jewels, and perfumes, poured into Europe from Syria and the East, and made living more full and rich. New methods of warfare were developed, together with a revival of siege machinery. The science of heraldry was fostered by the many knightly orders. Increased trade brought in its wake development in transport, in banking, and in use of bills of exchange. One evil result was the development of the sale of indulgences because all Crusaders were granted absolution. Culture and science were introduced on an ever-increasing scale with a corresponding broadening of outlook. Man began to look forward and upward—the world was getting ready for the metamorphosis from medieval to modern times.

Chapter XVII

The Protestant Revolt

At the beginning of the Middle Ages only about half Europe was Christian and the leadership of Rome was not yet recognized. By the middle of the period Christianity was widespread and the supremacy of the Pope was undisputed. At this time the Church made an honest attempt to provide spiritual leadership in a poverty economy. It taught men how to live amicably together and how to be worthy of better things to come. Inherently conservative, it did much to hamper scientific research. By the end of the Middle Ages a split had appeared between the north and the south, and Protestantism was a *fait accompli*.

England had been always recalcitrant and irked by the papal yoke. As early as the time of Henry II in the late twelfth century, the English kings had attacked unsuccessfully the Church courts. Parliament had curbed Church activity to a certain extent by the time of Henry VII in the late fifteenth century. John Wycliffe had appeared in the late fourteenth century, and his Lollard movement, although outlawed, continued unchecked. The English Church was weakened by its great wealth, which attracted many worldly people into the ranks of the clergy.

Under Henry VIII the real rift came. He asked the Pope to grant him a divorce from his first wife, Catherine, on the grounds that she had been first the wife of his older brother and that such a marriage with a brother's widow was forbidden. The Pope refused on the ground that the marriage had taken place under special dispensation. Henry tried to bring the Pope to his way of thinking by cutting off papal revenue and then by an Act of Parliament which forbade the appeal of any case to a court outside the realm. An English Church court then granted the annulment. In

1534 Henry went a step further by passing the Act of Supremacy. He thus became Supreme Head of the Church in England, received all the former papal revenue, and had the right of appointment of all English prelates. By 1536 if church officers would not recognize his leadership, they were convicted of treason. The next move against the Roman Church was confiscation of the property of monasteries and abbeys—of the smaller ones first, then of the larger, and finally even confiscation of shrines and images. It must be understood, however, that Henry was not a Protestant—he was Catholic—but simply took the Pope's authority to himself in his own kingdom.

Under Edward VI the confiscation and destruction of stained glass and images was completed. Edward also seized the funds which had been set up to pay for masses for the dead, and the right of appointment of bishops. He issued a new Prayer Book, containing forty-two articles of faith. Under Mary there was a nominal return to allegiance to the Pope, and we find severe persecution of heretics, with nearly three hundred executions.

Elizabeth came to the throne as the first Protestant sovereign, having Parliament establish the Church of England with the sovereign at its head. The Roman Catholic system of government was retained with archbishops, bishops, etc. Elizabeth did not hesitate to use persecution as a weapon, and it is estimated that more than two hundred were executed during her reign. The belief of the Church of England was set forth in a revised set of Thirty-Nine Articles, and a new Book of Common Prayer containing a prescribed order of services was authorized. The Mass was abolished and fines were imposed for attendance at Mass or for nonattendance at Anglican services. It was at this time that many Roman Catholics and many Protestant Dissenters—Baptists, Quakers, and Methodists—sought refuge and escape in America. Many of the colonies like Maryland and Pennsylvania were established primarily by these religious groups.

Protestantism first appeared in France in the fifteenth century along with the Renaissance. A renewed interest in the classics led Lefèvre, 1450–1537, to make a translation of the Bible into French directly from the Greek. He preached justification through faith long before Luther appeared in

Germany. By the middle of the sixteenth century, persecution of the Protestants was rampant in France, and many leaders like John Calvin fled to Switzerland. In spite of persecution, the Protestants, or Huguenots as they were called, increased in number and formed a strong political party under such leaders as Henry of Navarre and Coligny. In 1562 they gained permission by the Decree of Toleration to hold daylight meetings outside the towns. At the treacherous "Massacre of Vassy" one of these meetings was broken up and many Protestants were killed, leading to a civil religious war. Truce was called in 1570, but the perfidious nature of the peace was shown by an unsuccessful attempt to assassinate Coligny shortly afterward. The treacherous premeditated Massacre of St. Bartholomew's Day, August 23, 1572, is one of the blackest pages of Church history. Catherine of Medici, the queen mother, persuaded the king to kill the Huguenots while in Paris to attend the wedding celebration of Henry of Navarre and the king's sister. Estimates of the killings sometimes total as high as fifty thousand, but probably one-half or one-third of this number is more nearly correct.

The next open trouble was the so-called War of the Three Henrys. This turned out fortunately for the Huguenots. Henry III had Henry of Guise assassinated, the latter's followers then murdered the king, and Henry of Navarre automatically succeeded to the throne. In order to take the crown, he had to become a Catholic, but his famous jest, "So fair a kingdom is surely worth a Mass," is an indication of how serious his conversion was. Remembering his friends, he issued the Edict of Nantes in 1598, the first strong political move toward toleration, which was to remain in effect for nearly a century. Under this Edict the Calvinists were permitted to hold meetings anywhere except in Paris and certain other specified towns. They were granted equality of political rights. To ensure their enjoyment of these new-won privileges, the Huguenots were left in possession of certain fortified towns.

In Germany and Austria also, Protestantism took root. Luther, of whom more later, began the revolt here. Early in the sixteenth century, the Confession of Augsburg outlined the path the Reformation was to take. The Peace of Augsburg was an arrangement whereby the princes were given freedom of choice between Protestantism and Catholicism for the areas under their control. So important was the reform movement that in 1545 an ecumenical council—the Council of Trent—was called, which sat for nearly twenty years. Its object was chiefly to condemn the Protestant belief, but some of its reforms helped to strengthen the Church from within. The seven sacraments were ratified, the Vulgate version of the Bible was accepted as authoritative, and the supremacy of the Pope was recognized. It was this council that first instituted the "Index of Prohibited Books," a system of censorship still used by the Roman Catholic Church. The clergy were subjected to several reforms, their duty being emphasized. Protestantism continued to grow. The Treaty of Westphalia in 1648 at the end of the Thirty Years' War reiterated the Peace of Augsburg giving the rulers free choice of religion. In Austria, Joseph II in the late eighteenth century followed the pattern set by Henry VIII in England. He confiscated the monasteries, using the property for schools and charity. He forbade sending money to Rome, took to himself the appointment of bishops, and abolished the marriage sacrament, making marriage a civil ceremony by license. Frederick the Great was the first truly enlightened monarch in religious matters: he permitted complete freedom of choice of religion to his subjects. In the nineteenth century, Bismarck at first followed a policy of suppression of the Roman Catholics, but later, recognizing their importance as allies against socialism, he repealed the laws against the clergy and came to a cordial concordat with the Pope.

Chapter XVIII

The Growth of Tolerance

ENGLAND

THE early Stuarts in England were strong supporters of the church hierarchy, because the clergy supported their claims to rule by divine right. Their slogan, "No bishop, no king," became famous. They favored Catholicism, and appointed bishops to the Church of England who favored retention of Roman Catholic ritual and forms. Throughout their reign, there was growing opposition from the Separatists who sought religious toleration and were persecuted as anarchists, and from the Puritans who wished to "purify" the Church by abolishing the use of incense, altar, surplice, chants, and other reminders of the Roman Catholic ritual. When Archbishop Laud tried to enforce the use of the Book of Common Prayer in 1633, many Puritans fled, some finding their way to America. An attempt by the Stuarts to appoint bishops and clergy in the Scotch Presbyterian Church led to the Bishops' War in 1639. By 1640 the English Puritans, united with the country gentlemen, formed a party strong enough to plunge the country into civil war—a war which resulted in the beheading of Charles I and the establishment of a Protectorate under Oliver Cromwell.

The Restoration of the Stuarts in 1660 brought back the established church with no toleration for Dissenters. These Dissenters—Puritans, Independents, Baptists, and Quakers—now formed a large part of the community and brought much pressure to bear on the government in the struggle for toleration. They were instrumental in effecting a second revolution in 1688. This revolution brought with it considerable freedom of speech, thought, and religion. The bishops of the Church of England were appointed and paid by the government, but membership in the Established Church was no longer compulsory. The Act of Toleration, 1689, gave the Dissenters freedom of worship, but they were still barred from receiving degrees from universities and from sitting in Parliament. By the end of the seventeenth century there was very little persecution in England. Relations with Rome were completely broken, and Catholic Church property had been confiscated and used largely for schools. The Mass was still strictly prohibited, and Roman Catholics were prevented from immigrating to England and from holding any government or civil office in England. There was no censorship, and in practice there was little restraint of either Catholics or Dissenters.

In the eighteenth century a concession made in an obscure little French colony was to have echoes in nineteenth-century England. This was the Quebec Act of 1774 in Canada, which permitted the French-speaking colonists to practice the Roman Catholic religion. The Roman Catholics at home in England and those in Ireland immediately raised a clamor for toleration, arguing that if Catholicism should be permitted in a distant colony like Canada, it should also be permitted at home.

In 1828 the English Parliament repealed the laws against the Dissenters and admitted them to public office under oath that they would not use their influence to hurt the Established Church. The following year the Catholic Emancipation Act gave religious toleration to the Roman Catholics and permitted them to hold government and civil offices provided that they would take an oath renouncing the temporal supremacy of the Pope and disclaiming any intention of harming the Church of England. From that date there has been very little religious trouble in England. In 1870 when compulsory education was introduced there was a flurry of difficulty over what kind and how much of religious instruction should be given in the schools, but this soon was calmed.

English imperialist troubles in Ireland were aggravated by the religious problem. England had tried to force Protestantism on the Irish by way of the Church of England in Ireland. The monasteries and church lands had been seized and Protestant clergy substituted for the Catholic priests. The laws excluded the Catholics from Parliament, but they were forced to support the Established Church by taxes. Collection of this tithe was difficult and dangerous, often leading to fierce local battles. The first relief came with the Catholic Emancipation Act cited above. By 1868 Gladstone, with the help of Catholics in Parliament, was able to have the English Church in Ireland "disestablished" and its tithes abolished. As compensation, the Church was allowed to retain its buildings and property, and received a large government grant in lieu of tithes. This victory for the Irish had far-reaching effects in giving added impetus to the agitation for land reform and home rule.

FRANCE

There was but little corresponding religious trouble in France until late in the seventeenth century. In 1682 the Declaration of the Liberties of the Gallican Church was promulgated, by which the Pope was granted full supremacy in religious matters but was relieved of all temporal power in France. This resulted in a deadlock between king and Pope for nearly twelve years until Louis XIV gained the right to appoint the lower clergy in return for permitting the bishops to renounce the Declaration of 1682. The Declaration, however, was still a part of French law and meant that the French king retained a good deal of authority over the French Church. Louis XIV was a strong Catholic and undertook to suppress the Huguenots. He began by demolishing their churches and orphanages, Huguenot orphans thus being forced into the care of Catholic guardians. The Huguenots were excluded from public office and from the legal and medical professions. They were forbidden to write books. If they refused to accept the Roman Catholic Church they had soldiers quartered upon them. In 1685 the Edict of Nantes was revoked, thus exiling Huguenot ministers, closing their schools, and forbidding public worship to them. Many Protestants fled to the New World to escape such persecution, taking with them their skills, knowledge, industry, and money—an incalculable loss to France. Those who chose to remain were hunted, imprisoned, killed, or sent to the galleys.

Protestants had no civil rights after this date and were practically outlawed, with no registration of births, deaths, or marriages. After 1724 all non-Catholics who met for public worship were subject to confiscation of their estates. Any minister holding other than Catholic services was condemned to death on summary conviction.

By the eighteenth century, two strong men had appeared as champions of toleration. Diderot in his *Encyclopaedia*, published in spite of Church opposition, attacked religious intolerance and encouraged men to follow natural science rather than theology. Voltaire, in his ironic, pointed way, showed the Church to be the greatest obstacle to the exercise of reason, to progress, and to enlightenment. Voltaire is often cited as an example of an atheist or enemy of religion, but he was strongly religious—only opposing and ridiculing any organization, including the Church, which opposed freedom of thought.

The eighteenth-century clergy had many privileges. Deriving their authority from the Church and being much better organized than the nobles, they had a powerful influence on the government. They still possessed gorgeous ceremonial, vast wealth and property. Their intolerance of those who disagreed was extreme, refusal to recognize the Church being the equivalent in their eyes of treason against God. They managed the schools, charities, and hospitals. Church courts could exact fines or impose imprisonment. The clergy registered all births and deaths, and sanctified marriage. Themselves exempt from any direct taxation, they exacted large tithes. A commission under the Pope watched all publications for subversive writings, and placed these freely on the "Index." Likewise, they clamped down a close censorship on teachings at the various universities, thus retarding scientific research. Many of the bishops ruled as temporal princes. Protected by the Inquisition and censorship, the Church flourished up to the time of the French Revolution. By that time there were demands for redress from the clergy themselves—the higher clergy because they were losing privileges and prestige, and the lesser clergy because the tithe was not used locally but poured into a central treasury. It is generally estimated that, when the Revolution came, the First Estate was composed of one hundred and thirty thousand Roman Catholic clergy, possessing about one-fifth the land of France.

The French Revolution brought tremendous changes. One clause in the *Declaration of the Rights of Man* in 1789 states, "No one shall be disquieted on account of his opinions, including his religious views, provided their manifestation does not disturb the public order established by law." The tithe was abolished. The National Assembly in 1790 took away all special privileges of the clergy and granted freedom of religion to all whether Catholic, Protestant, or Jew. The clergy were now simple citizens subject to the regular civil law. Their right of censorship was cancelled. All Church property was confiscated by the state. Because the Catholic Church had been so strong, the Revolutionaries were afraid to leave it on an equal level with the others and tried to nationalize it. The bishops and clergy, like all civil officials, were to gain office by popular election and to be paid by the government. The Pope had no authority over this new Church, but by the Civil Constitution of the Clergy, July 1790, he was allowed to define belief and doctrine. The chief duty of the new church was to teach those practical moral virtues thought necessary for the making of good citizens. One result of this reorganization of the church was to stir up the opposition of the clergy to the Revolution.

The attempt to destroy the Roman Catholic Church in France proved a failure. Napoleon recognized the importance of a strong church as a power in politics and made his peace with the Pope in the Concordat of 1801. All priests and nonjuring clergy were freed on the promise of not opposing the constitution. Sunday was restored along with the old calendar. The Pope was recognized as head of the Church and popular election of the clergy was abandoned. The election of the bishops was to be in the hands of the emperor, but they were then given authority to appoint the lesser clergy. Church property was not restored, and religious tolerance was maintained in France. Napoleon also definitely separated school and Church by instituting a public-school system in France. However, under Napoleon III the Church regained some control of education.

The Third Republic in France proposed to establish liberty of conscience, freedom of speech, press, and religion, separation of Church and State, and nonreligious education. All of this was opposed by Pope Pius IX in his *Syllabus of Errors*; so from the first there was opposition to the new Republic by the clergy. The Jesuits and the Church schools were accused of teaching distrust of the republican government; religious newspapers referred to the new Republic as "an unfortunate accident"; and the clericals were charged with instigating a movement to restore the monarchy. The anticlericals organized their efforts and made their aim threefold: to remove control of the clergy from the schools, to stop government payment of the salaries of the clergy, and to separate Church and state.

Between 1881 and 1886 compulsory education was established for children of six to thirteen. Primary education was to be free, and no clergyman could be hired as a teacher in a public school. Many religious orders had been re-established since the first revolution, and the Association Law of 1901 was passed to prevent the continuance of religious orders without a license and to forbid members of unlicensed associations to teach. This law resulted in the closing of about ten thousand Church schools and in the complete control of education by the state.

In 1895, the first move was made to separate Church and state and to stop government payment of clergy salaries. The Concordat of 1801 was revived. In 1905 the Separation Law finally separated Church and state and stopped all government appropriation for religious purposes. Clergy of long service were granted pensions, and all others had their salaries stopped by a graduated cut over a short period. All Church property, including cathedrals and bishops' residences, was declared owned by the government. Many residences and seminaries were turned into hospitals and schools, but the government permitted the use of all church buildings for public worship free of charge. The Church was allowed to choose its own prelates without government interference. At first the clergy refused to accept the terms, but when they found the government backed by the people, they capitulated as gracefully as possible. Thus, practically in our own day, was tolerance achieved in France.

Chapter XIX

Notes on the Great Reformers

WE have already referred to the "Doctors" or Fathers of the early Church—Gregory, Innocent, Augustine, Boniface, and others. As schisms emerged, other "fathers" appeared who founded new sects free from the domination of the Pope. Some of these did more important work than was done by any political group to free men's minds, and return a large portion of the Christian world to reliance on the Bible rather than the Church.

WYCLIFFE

One of the earliest of these religious discoverers, if they may be so called, was an Englishman, John Wycliffe, born about 1320 at Hipwell, Yorkshire. Educated at Oxford, he became master of Balliol College in 1360. A zealous reformer of clerical abuses, he supported Parliament in its defiance of the Pope, blamed the wealth of the Church for many of the evils found therein, proposed that the Bible should be the final authority in matters of religion, and proclaimed that man needed no priest as an intermediary to God. The Great Schism in the Church served to emphasize his point that the Pope was unnecessary.

To facilitate use of the Bible, he began a translation of it into English in 1378. This translation became the basis of all later English translations and was so well done that Wycliffe has been known since as the father of English prose. By the time the translation was completed he had gathered a band of Oxford scholars about him, who became the nucleus of the Lollard movement. Dressed in coarse redwoollen cloth, barefoot, and staff in hand, these "poor preachers" moved about the country preaching their new doctrine to the poor and lowly classes.

Basing their beliefs on their own interpretation of the Bible, the Lollards denounced veneration of saints, fasting, indulgences, pardons, and use of images—as useless attributes of the Church. They accepted the Augustinian theory of predestination, thus making salvation dependent on grace rather than merit. The doctrines of confession and transubstantiation were rejected.

The Church sought to destroy the Lollards as dangerous heretics. More than once John Wycliffe was saved from the canonical authorities by the London mob. The Lollards were charged with stirring up the discontent that resulted in the Peasant's War, and this charge detracted from their following. However, Lollardy was still on the increase when Wycliffe died in 1384.

HUS

John Hus, born about 1369 in Husinetz, Bohemia, and educated at the University of Prague, early came under the influence of John Wycliffe. He carried the Lollard movement to Prague, and it soon became widespread in Bohemia. For criticizing Church doctrine and opposing the sale of indulgences, he was excommunicated in 1412. It has already been mentioned that the Pope offered him a safe-conduct to the Council of Constance to defend his beliefs. In good faith he attended the council, but once he was arrived the Church ignored the safe-conduct, tried him for heresy, and burned him at the stake in 1415. Thus did Hus become one of the earliest Protestant martyrs.

ERASMUS

Desiderius Erasmus was an illegitimate child born in Rotterdam, Holland, in 1465. It is reported that his name was a Greek-Latin translation of that of his father. In 1486 he became an Augustinian friar. He travelled extensively, visiting several of the European courts. A scholar rather than a theologian, he attacked the usage of many of the Latin classical writers. He wrote a book of maxims from the classics, and enlivened it with his own comment. Very early he expressed a belief that the Bible should be translated into the vernacular. He did not make such a translation him-self, but he did publish an edition of the New Testament in Greek, with a Latin translation and commentary placed in parallel columns with it. He attacked formal religion, claiming that the two great enemies of religion were pagan-ism and a belief in outward forms and ceremonies. He be-lieved that Church dogma and law killed the very essence of religion, which was harmony and peace. He criticized the vices of the priests and attacked most of the abuses later opposed by Martin Luther. He saw the necessity for reform in the Church and thought that the time was ripe for it while there were "enlightened despots" on the thrones of Europe. However, he wanted gradual reform through edu-cation, and always opposed the violence displayed by Luther. He died at Basel, Switzerland, in 1536.

ZWINGLI

Ulrich Zwingli was born at Wildhaus, Switzerland, in 1484. He was educated at Berne, Basel, and Vienna, and was ordained to the priesthood in 1506. By 1518 he was pastor at Zurich. His studies caused him to question the authority of the Pope, and he began to attack both religious and social evils such as the sale of indulgences and the traffic in mercenary soldiers. Probably he preached the doctrine of justification by faith before Martin Luther. These two con-temporary reformers could not agree on the interpretation of the Eucharist, Zwingli claiming it to be only a symbol whereas Luther preferred to cling to the older doctrine of transubstantiation. Zwingli fell in battle at Cappel in 1531.

LUTHER

Martin Luther is probably the best-known name among the religious reformers. He was born into a poor family at Eisleben, Germany, in 1483. In spite of poverty, he was edu-cated at Magdeburg, Eisenach, and the University of Er-furt, where to please his father he studied law. After com-pletion of the law course, he decided to become a monk, and in 1509 he began to teach Aristotle at the University of Wittenberg. He feared that he himself was going to Hell, and only after several years of internal struggle did he arrive at the conclusion that one could achieve salvation by faith—a doctrine which he soon began to preach in his classes.

All was well until 1517 when a transient priest, John Tezel, appeared in Wittenberg and began the sale of indulgences. This sale of indulgences was becoming a nuisance in the Church—there was no repentance for sin required, but for confession and the payment of a certain variable sum one could obtain a remission of purgatorial suffering. Tezel so provoked Luther that he drew up and posted on the door of the Wittenberg Church a series of ninety-five theses attacking and condemning certain evils and abuses in the Church, including the sale of indulgences. These theses were published in Latin and Luther intended that they should be used as a basis for discussion by scholars like himself, but they were translated into German and scattered far and wide throughout the country. In the course of the next three years, Luther found himself at the crest of a great wave of popularity among the common people, the leader of a great reform movement. Germany was in the midst of its first great war of pamphleteers.

The Pope at first chose to ignore Luther, but his movement seemed to be spreading and so in 1519 Dr. Eck was sent to confute him. In his debate with Eck, Luther stated his beliefs clearly. He said that he believed every man could interpret the Bible for himself; that he could approach God without the assistance of the priest as an intermediary; that justification came through faith, not good works; that the early apostles knew nothing of masses, purgatory, pilgrimage, indulgences, or political headship of the Pope. In June of 1520 he was warned to recant and make his peace with the Church, but this he refused to do, and publicly burned the papal bull against himself. This act led to his excommunication in January, 1521.

In the summer of the same year he was summoned to the Diet of Worms. Here he was again asked to recant. When he refused, his books were publicly burned and he was outlawed. The Elector of Saxony, to save his life, kidnapped him and took him into voluntary imprisonment at the Wartburg for a year. While in Wartburg Castle, he made the first good translation of the New Testament into German, and started a movement to write in German prose.

In 1522 he returned to his teaching at Wittenberg, and he remained there till his death in 1546. For a time he clung to the idea of reforming the Roman Catholic Church from within. Eventually he abandoned this hope and formed the German Evangelical (Lutheran) Church. In 1525 he married a former nun, and his married life reveals his softer and better side. An extremely violent man, he showed many faults and limitations, but his tact and tenderness were also on a grand scale.

Luther recognized the fact that religious reform meant social reform also. Unlike Erasmus, he did not believe that man was a free agent who would get better and better with education. In his *Address to the German Nobility* he proposed a threefold attack on the Church: first, against the idea that the clergy were a separate class entitled to special privileges and subject to special regulations; second, against the idea that the Pope superseded the Church councils in authority; and third, against the right of the Pope to be sole interpreter of the Scriptures. He called for a five-point program of social reform to bolster this attack: one, reduction of the number of monasteries; two, remaining monasteries to be used as hospitals and houses of refuge; three, marriage of the clergy; four, reduction of Church holidays and pilgrimages, which had become so numerous that they interfered with daily work; five, reform of the universities to stress research and freedom from Aristotelian authority.

The followers of the new sect were numerous and ranged from the lowliest to the highest. The common people accepted his doctrine because they were tired of the worldliness of the clergy, of observance of only forms in worship, and of abuses such as indulgences. They now had the Bible in their own hands and wished to escape the oppression of the Church. The clergy followed Luther readily in order to escape their monastic vows, and the rulers welcomed the opportunity to seize some Church property. Luther always preached against violence, but the new machine could not be controlled by the driver and there was trouble— the rulers revolted against the Church leaders, the clergy against the Church ritual, and the peasants against oppression. When the peasant movement was suppressed with great violence, probably at the instigation of Luther, who was never a democrat, he was greatly discredited.

The first approach to settlement came in 1526 at the Diet of Speyer. Every German ruling prince and every free town was given freedom of choice between the Roman Catholic and the Evangelical Church for the regions under his or its control—note that this did not mean religious freedom for the individual. When a second Diet of Speyer, 1529, tried to enforce the rulings of the Diet of Worms against heretics, the dissenting rulers drew up a *protest*, hence for the first time the term "Protestant." The following year, the Diet of Augsburg asked each side to draw up a statement of its fundamental doctrines. The Evangelical Church presented what was to become famous as the "Augsburg Confession"—the doctrine of Luther written up by Melanchthon. This was to be the creed of the Lutheran Evangelical Church, and it put forth the same fundamental view of Christianity as the Roman Catholic Church but rejected some Catholic practices. After another quarter-century of conflict the Peace of Augsburg, 1555, finally established the arrangement made at the first Diet of Speyer.

Lutheranism has always been on the conservative side in reform. It was always oligarchic and governed from above, never democratic like Calvinism. Emphasis was placed on congregational participation in the services, and more freedom of worship was allowed than formerly. Today there are perhaps seventy million members of the Lutheran Evangelical Church.

CALVIN

John Calvin was born at Noyon, France, in 1509. Coming from a good family, he was educated at the University of Paris and the University of Orleans. At first he started to train for the priesthood, but he later changed to law, for which his logical mind admirably suited him. Being influenced by Luther, he avowed Protestantism in 1533 and soon rose to a position of leadership in the movement, becoming one of the signatories of the Augsburg Confession. To escape persecution at home, he removed to Basel and later to Geneva, where he held high civil positions. The close union of church and state under his direction led to a strict moral code enforced by severe civil penalties, but too stringent disciplinary measures defeat their own ends and Calvin found himself banished from Geneva for a time.

As a civil administrator he had reduced poverty, improved health conditions, and developed trade. In church organization he developed a new democratic system with election of all church officers by the congregation, and by having some posts occupied by laymen. The term "Presbyterian" was applied to this new group, from the use of the word "presbyter" for pastor or priest. Calvinism appealed mainly to the middle-class businessman because of its encouragement of hard work, thrift, good management, plain living, and high thinking.

Calvin gave Protestantism an organized system which kept it strong through the sixteenth and seventeenth centuries. He was always frank and sincere, and able to back his principles with sound reasoning. His *Institutes of the Christian Religion* is really the first well-ordered treatise on Protestant belief based on the supreme authority of the Bible and the doctrine of justification by faith. His French translation of the Bible is outstanding, and reveals his logical, legally-trained mind. He died in 1564, but his movement lived on.

KNOX

Calvinism was carried to Scotland by John Knox. Knox was born about 1514 at Haddington, Scotland. Educated at Haddington and the University of Glasgow, he took minor orders. After his conversion to Protestantism in 1545 he spent much time on the Continent, and there he made contact with John Calvin. Calvinistic emphasis on good management, thrift, and hard work appealed to his canny Scotch mind, and when he returned home he carried with him Presbyterianism. He was a shrewd, earnest, and powerful preacher of the new belief, and his *Confession of Faith*, written for Scotch Protestants, is a clear-cut statement of his fundamental teachings. Also a social reformer, he made an attempt shortly before his death in 1572 to divert the old church revenues into new channels, for the promotion of social welfare and intellectual and religious revival, but in this he was balked by the nobles.

WESLEY

John Wesley was one of the latest of the great reformers, not appearing on the scene until the eighteenth century. Born at Epworth, England, in 1703, the son of a minister, he was sent to Charterhouse School for Boys; Christ Church, Oxford; and Lincoln College. Not much interested in religion at first, he became an ordained Church of England minister in 1728, and he was placed as a tutor at Lincoln College. In the same year that he was ordained he and his brother Charles organized the Holy Club of Methodists at Oxford, so-called because of their piety and regularity of habits. In 1735 John Wesley came to America, where he was greatly impressed by the simple faith of the Moravians in Georgia.

Returning to England in 1737, he felt himself "called of God" to preach a new doctrine, and within a few years Methodism had spread throughout Britain and America. The Methodists made sudden conversion and complete forgiveness of sins the foundation of their teachings. Wesley was a spellbinding preacher with a genius for organizing. He used his private income from the sale of his books very lavishly to spread the new belief. The press was skilfully exploited with his propaganda. Realizing that social reform would give impetus to his movement, he provided work for the unemployed, did welfare work among the armed services, and opened dispensaries for distribution of medicines and the spread of health information. He helped organize the Methodist Episcopal Church in America in 1784, and before his death in 1791 the break with the Church of England was almost complete.

At his death, he left a declaration establishing the Methodist Church with one hundred named ministers as a governing body. Vacancies in this body were to be filled by election, and for many years the governing body was composed of ministers only. Today there are two divisions in the conference: the pastoral, made up of ministers only, to

discuss and clarify doctrine and policy, and a second body of
both ministers and laymen to consider matters of finance.
The modern church is a center of social welfare work. It
has its own seminaries, colleges, and normal schools for
training preachers and teachers. The itineracy of the clergy
has been maintained, a minister but rarely holding a post
for more than three years.

Chapter XX

Later Movements

THE QUAKERS

THE Society of Friends, or Quakers, was founded by George Fox in 1647. It aimed at the restoration of a primitive Christian religion. The Quakers were distinguished from other sects by their simplicity of life, dress, and ritual. All ceremonial, including even the Lord's Supper, was abolished. They were the first organization to denounce the use of war as an instrument of international policy, and have always been prominent in peace movements.

The founder, George Fox, was born of middle-class parents in 1624. The England of that day was stirred by internal trouble which flared into the Civil War while Fox was still a boy. Free speech was a thing unknown. A man of fine natural intelligence, he made the most of his middle-class education. In his early twenties he claimed to have received a revelation, and began to call men to a life exemplary of the indwelling light and power of Christ. He rescued Christianity from the hands of the theologians and again emphasized it as a way of life rather than a ceremonial. He opposed both the High-Church professors who clung to ancient tradition and the Puritans who clung to Scripture. He removed the emphasis from the expiatory death of Christ to the living Christ in the human heart.

The Ten Talents of Quakerism are as follows:

1. God's spiritual light, lightening every man.
2. The indwelling of the Spirit with the disciple.
3. The headship of Christ in the church.
4. The priesthood of all true believers—note their meetings where none acts as priest, but all sit quietly until some member of the congregation is moved "by the spirit" to speak.

5. The freedom of the Gospel ministry.
6. The spiritual equality of the sexes.
7. Spiritual baptism and spiritual communion only—no sacraments whatsoever.
8. The unlawfulness of war.
9. The unlawfulness of oaths.
10. The duty of brotherly love and simplicity of life.

Quakerism was transplanted to the New World by William Penn, and the Quakers settled in what was to become known as the "Quaker State," Pennsylvania. Major emphasis was placed on the individual conscience. There is a noticeably diminished spirit of self-seeking or personal ambition among these people. They did their duty in everyday life, and were seen to do their duty. From early colonial times, the term "Quaker" has been synonymous with honesty and square dealing.

THE DEISTS

Deism had its main growth after the Reformation. It is a natural system of religion, based on science and logic, and opposed both to atheism, which denies the existence of God, and to any religious system based on a belief in a God who reveals himself to man. It is thus antagonistic to Christianity, Mohammedanism, Buddhism, and Pantheism.

The Deists have three canons and four major beliefs, the seven together being a substitute for a creed. The four beliefs are as follows: first, there is one God, supreme over the universe in power, wisdom, and goodness, but he does not and cannot reveal himself to man; second, the world is now ordered for the best, and since it is working for the best, the end will be good; third, life will be continued forever and immortality is assured, because God loves his creation and would not part with it (the fact that man has life at all is an evidence of God's love); and fourth, God is a constant, powerful stimulant to highest virtue and brotherly love, not simply an intellectual conviction.

The leading canon states that it is the right and duty of every man to think for himself on matters of religion. No outside influence, book, man, or church may be used as an authority binding on the individual mind and conscience.

The second canon tells us that all professed knowledge of God is partial, defective, and insignificant, but that such knowledge can be increased, corrected, and refined by proper use of our faculties of reason, love, conscience, and religion. The third canon clearly emphasizes the point that all knowledge of God must be based on natural, immutable facts in the phenomena of nature. No Deistic belief is at variance with established conclusions of science.

Since Deism is based on indisputable fact, it is capable of expansion and elevation with every increase in knowledge of the universe. It is a belief in a God who exacts strict obedience, but to obey whom is not a hardship because he can be thoroughly loved and trusted. The Deist tests revelation by the four faculties mentioned above, and points out that any revelation cannot be accepted by one or more of these faculties. Part of the Scriptures, such as the Psalms in the Old Testament and moral precepts in the New Testament are accepted for their intrinsic value, but not for any revelatory reason. Much of the Christian New Testament is opposed on the ground that it is irrational, clearly false, and morally objectionable. The Deist reasons that God must be at least as good as the best of men and therefore a revengeful or penal hell is impossible.

The Deist admits that the faculty of reason alone is incapable of explaining the phenomena of life, growth, decay, and destruction, or of solving the riddle of good and evil. Therefore, we have the second faculty, conscience or moral sense, a voice within us which tells us to do good because it is good and to avoid evil because it is evil. This moral sense precludes any desire for reward or fear of punishment. Pain and death are not regarded as intrinsically evil, but as essentials to happiness and progress—pain for cleansing from, not punishment for, sin; and death as the porchway or entrance gate into a higher state of life.

To perfect these two faculties, we have a third, Love. This is a source of joy, and because it is entirely unselfish, it permits us to do our duty to our fellow and have happiness at the same time. It is the conqueror of the world's evil, and makes its possessor able and willing to bear whatever happens.

Deism is not simply an intellectual conception but it is

a practical religion. Because of its basis in reason it has great appeal for the modern intellectual. Its recognition of God as an All-father makes all men brethren and thus emphasizes the Christian ideal expressed in Christ's second commandment. The Deist could not reasonably follow any other course than the Golden Rule.

THE MORMONS

The Church of Jesus Christ of Latter-day Saints is usually, though erroneously, called "Mormon" because of the belief in the divine authenticity of the Book of Mormon. The creed outlines a belief in the revelation of God to his children: that since God is invariable and no respecter of persons his laws are immutable, and that whatsoever he gives by revelation is a law to the Saints. Their Thirteen Articles of Faith may be outlined as follows:

"1. We believe in God the Eternal Father, in his son Jesus Christ, and in the Holy Ghost.

"2. We believe that man will be punished for his own sins only, and not for Adam's transgression.

"3. We believe that all mankind can be saved through the atonement of Christ by obedience to the laws and ordinances of the Gospels.

"4. We believe that these ordinances are faith in the Lord Jesus Christ, repentance, baptism by immersion for remission of sins, and laying on of hands for the gift of the Holy Ghost.

"5. We believe that a man must be called of God, by prophecy, and by laying on of hands by those in authority, to preach the Gospel and administer its ordinances.

"6. We believe in the same organization as existed in the primitive church—apostles, prophets, pastors, teachers, evangelists, deacons.

"7. We believe in the gifts of tongues, of interpretation of tongues, of prophecy, of visions, of revelation, of healing by faith.

"8. We believe the Bible to be the Word of God insofar as it is correctly translated; we also believe the Book of Mormon to be the Word of God.

"9. We believe all that God has revealed, all that he does

now reveal; and we believe He will yet reveal many great and important things concerning the Kingdom of God.

"10. We believe literally in the gathering of Israel and the restoration of the Ten Tribes; that Zion will be built upon this continent; that Christ will personally reign on this earth; that the earth will be renewed and receive its paradisiac glory.

"11. We claim the right of worshipping Almighty God according to the dictates of our conscience, and allow all men the same privilege, let them worship how, where, or what they may.

"12. We believe in being subject to kings, rulers, presidents, and magistrates; in obeying, honoring, and sustaining the law of the state in which we live.

"13. We believe in being honest, true, chaste, benevolent, virtuous, and in doing good to all men."

Joseph Smith, the founder, was born of farming people at Sharon, Vermont, December 23, 1805. When a boy of fifteen he became deeply interested in religion, and continuing faithful he believed himself to receive messengers from Heaven. Of these, the angel Moroni was chief, and he revealed to the boy the knowledge of the existence and whereabouts of the Book of Mormon. Smith continued to receive these heavenly visits, and his "dreams" resulted in much persecution and even attempts on his life. After he had received sufficient instruction and visitation, the Book of Mormon was entrusted to his care with a key for its translation.

Moroni revealed that he had buried the sacred record in the year 420 in the hill Cumorah in northern New York State. It was an abridgment made by Mormon, father of Moroni, from the records of his forefathers, and hence the name. The Urim and Thummim which Joseph Smith was to use as keys were described as two transparent stones set in the rim of a bow attached to a breastplate. The Book itself was a volume of plates about six inches thick bound together by three rings, with a part of it sealed. Each plate was about six inches by eight inches, not quite as thick as ordinary tin sheets, covered with engraved Egyptian characters. It showed many marks of antiquity in construction, and exquisite workmanship in the engraving, even of the smallest characters. Joseph Smith translated the unsealed portion, which was published in 1830 as the "Book of Mormon," and the whole was again taken in charge by the angel.

Smith and his followers maintain that in 1829 Smith was ordained by John the Baptist and made an apostle. On 1830, April 6th, the Church of Jesus Christ of Latter-day Saints was established at Fayette, New York, with Joseph Smith its first prophet. Members were ordained to go out and preach, and the new belief spread rapidly. A temple was built at Kirtland, Ohio; Missouri became a center; Nauvoo, Illinois, was the headquarters for another group. They met popular disfavor and persecution in many quarters, largely because plurality of wives was permitted. Continued persecution drove them farther and farther westward. Smith was assassinated in Carthage jail, June 27, **1844**, and the presidency descended to Brigham Young. To avoid further persecution, the latter agreed to leave Illinois, but by some miscarriage of justice, after part of the Nauvoo settlement had already started to move, the balance was attacked and annihilated. In the fifteen-hundred-mile trek to the basin of Great Salt Lake the Mormons lost another thousand of their followers. Here they dwelt for a time in peace and established the great temple of Salt Lake City. In 1850 the Territory of Utah was organized as part of the United States of America, and in 1857 through some misrepresentation an army was dispatched to disperse the Mormons. It was recalled, however; and since that time the Mormons have felt no further persecution.

In 1952 there were over one million followers, dispersed in three hundred districts, or Stakes of Zion, extending from southern Alberta to the northern boundary of Mexico. The hierarchy of the church is so extensive that practically every male is in some way connected with the church organization. They follow the law of the country, including the regulation of monogamous marriage. A chief criticism of the sect is their attitude toward women, but this has improved since monogamous marriage has been enforced. They call on all men to do the will of God, and seem to have solved the problem of a happy, prosperous, and contented life.

CHRISTIAN SCIENCE

Mary Baker Eddy was the founder. She held that in 1866 after reading Matt. 9:1–8 she had been almost miraculously healed of a severe injury. From that time on she sought knowledge re the science of this healing. Her findings are a religious teaching based on the words and works of Jesus Christ—in her own words, "a scientific system of divine healing." In 1875 her principle work was published, *Science and Health with a Key to the Scriptures*. She set up the Church of Christ, Scientist, in Boston in 1879, later establishing there in 1892 a mother church, The First Church of Christ, Scientist.

The theology starts with the idea that God is the only mind. A sharp distinction is drawn between the real and the apparent but unreal. It teaches that all evil and error is to be overcome on the basis of its unreality. Part of the rule is found in John 8:32, "Ye shall know the truth, and the truth shall make you free." The practice of Christian Science is both a mental and a spiritual discipline. The practitioner must prepare for the healing ministry—healing of all evils, not sickness alone—by living the genuine Christian life. Mrs. Eddy passed away in 1910, but her work was carried on by a board of directors established by her *Church Manual*. Today there are more than 3,000 Christian Science churches; 2,251 of them in the United States.

UNITARIANISM

The name is derived from the doctrine of the single personality of God instead of the more popular idea of the Trinity. The movement began in the late seventeenth century, rejecting the whole Trinitarian scheme of salvation with its doctrines of inherited sin, eternal punishment, and atonement. The movement is marked by its demand for personal religious freedom and by its rejection of all creeds, going back to the Bible as the only source of belief. Some of the better known leaders were William Ellery Channing, Theodore Parker, Ralph Waldo Emerson, and J. Hamilton Thom. The sect later came to accept not only the Bible, but also religious history and experience interpreted by conscience and reason. Growth of various branches was largely independent, but several of the larger groups united in 1928 in the "General Assembly of Unitarian and Free Christian Churches." At that time, there were about four hundred churches on this continent.

SOME MISCELLANEOUS GROUPS

The *Mennonites* were founded by Menno Simons at Zurich about 1525. They were an offshoot of the Anabaptists, being opposed to infant baptism and substituting therefore a baptism of believers after the age of reason is reached. They accept no authority outside the Bible, reject the death penalty, abstain from all oaths, and are conscientious objectors to military service. In 1940, there were an estimated 175,000 Mennonites in Canada and United States.

Spiritualism is a belief that the activity of humankind is not limited to the use they make of their bodily organs on this earth, but that an animating principle or spirit has entered matter to develop a personality which may continue with all its attributes after the matter has worn out, and that under certain limitations this personality can guide or influence terrestrial affairs through the medium of the living.

Bahá'i was founded by Baha'u'llah (1817–92). He taught that revelation was continuous, and that the divine command for our age is unification of mankind under one faith. There are at present about 500 communities in Persia and upwards of 169 in this continent.

Chapter XXI

Recent Developments in Italy, Germany, and U.S.S.R.

ITALY

WHEN Italy was unified in 1870, the whole papal holdings, with the exception of the Vatican Palace, were seized by the new government. For sixty years the Popes considered themselves prisoners of the Italian state and remained in voluntary confinement in the palace. Finally, in 1929, Mussolini arranged a series of negotiations with Pope Pius XI resulting in three agreements—a treaty, a financial agreement, and a concordat.

The Vatican State, comprising an area of one hundred acres with a population of five hundred, was recognized as an autonomous state under the sovereignty of the Pope. This territory was to be forever neutral and inviolable, and the entrance was to be guarded by Swiss. The tiny state has its own coinage and postage and its own diplomatic corps, appointing and receiving ambassadors. The Pope recognized the independence of the Kingdom of Italy from his temporal authority and received in return an indemnity from the Italian government of nearly ninety-two million dollars. Roman Catholicism was recognized as the Italian state religion, and the government undertook to enforce canon law. Religious education was made compulsory in both the elementary and secondary schools. Probably one of the reasons for such a congenial arrangement was to be found in the fact that both the government and the Church were powerful opponents of communism.

In postwar Italy, the Roman Catholic Church continues to be militantly anti-Communist. Opposition to Protestant church organizations often takes the form of the implication that Protestantism and Communism are linked together. The Protestant churches retort that much of Italy's continuing poverty results from oppression by the Roman Catholic Church. Protestant organizations are experiencing difficulty getting the legal freedom granted by the Italian constitution, and some highly placed Protestant clergy are calling upon the Roman Catholic Church to give the same freedom of religious conviction to minorities in Italy that they themselves expect to receive in countries where they are in the minority. The deportation from Italy of Rex Paden in 1955, after some eight years of work as an organizer of the evangelistic Church of Christ, is indicative of the enmity between the Roman Catholic hierarchy and the burgeoning Protestant movement.

GERMANY

The official National Socialist (Nazi) Party program stated that it stood for a positive Christianity without binding itself to any confession. From the first it took a stand against the organized churches, both Catholic and Protestant. Probably the official view was best expressed by Rosenberg in his *Myth of the Twentieth Century*, which was required reading for all members of the Nazi party and is one of the few books on the Roman Catholic "Index" today.

Rosenberg outlined a "religion of Blood" or Race, setting forth a belief in the supremacy of Germanic man. To fit this mold, Christianity had to be purged of every trace of Judaism. The Old Testament was to be abolished and replaced by a collection of Nordic sagas. The "superstitious" parts of the New Testament were to be rejected, and the teachings about human brotherhood and humility were to be revised. The crucifix was discarded, together with a belief in Christ as the "Lamb" of God. A new register of martyrs and "saints of the Blood" was composed of Germany's World War I heroes.

The creed of Nazi Germany ran as follows: "I believe in the God of the German religion, who is at work in nature; in the noble Spirit of Man; and in the struggle of my people. I believe in the helper-in-need, Christ, who fights for the 'nobility of man, and in Germany where the new humanity is being created." Baldur von Schirach proceeded to instill the idea of a state religion in the two Nazi youth movements, the Hitler Youth and the Federation of German Girls. He exhorted them: "Stand together. Fight for Adolf Hitler. Fight for our German Fatherland. If you do this, then are you fulfilling the will of God."

These "German Christians" took a strong stand against the organized churches, against the Jews, and against Marxism. They wished to cleanse the German Church of everything "un-German," including the Old Testament. The government openly took sides to support the Neopagans. Priests were discredited before the public by charges of trying to smuggle money out of the Reich, later by charges of immorality—especially the monastic orders. Legal force could be used against the Roman Catholic priests because they were invariably opposed to the new sterilization laws applying to all physical, mental, or "racial" defectives.

The attempt to unify all the Protestant Churches under a single Reichsbishop was a flagrant attempt to subjugate the German Protestants. It resulted only in unifying opposition to the German Christians. Leaders like Niemöller in the German Evangelical (Lutheran) Church and Karl Barth in the German Reformed (Calvinist) Church made their appearance. Adolf Hitler's choice for the post of Reichsbishop was Mueller, and he was given the use of newspapers and radio facilities which were denied to Niemöller, the choice of the churches. The struggle resulted in the dismissal or imprisonment of many of the clergy. Niemöller was imprisoned, tried, and released in 1937, but almost immediately rearrested and taken to a concentration camp without any charge being laid.

Attacks on the Catholic Church were more open, because this church opposed the basic principles of a totalitarian state. The Catholic Center Party was abolished soon after Adolf Hitler came to power in 1933. Catholic Youth movements found their members constantly molested by the Hitler Youth. Many Roman Catholics fell victims of Nazi terror. As reports grew in volume that the Hitler Youth was becoming anti-Christian and pagan, any priests who opposed them were immediately jailed. The Catholic schools were attacked so energetically that by 1936 enrollments were halved, and on January 1, 1937, all members of religious orders in state-supported schools were dismissed. After 1937 a workingman had to be a member of the Labor Front in order to secure or hold a job, and Catholic workingmen's groups were forbidden membership.

Most to be feared is the neopagan influence inculcated in the Hitler Youth. This youth movement grew constantly during the Nazi regime. The only other youth movement in Germany was the Catholic Youth, and this was systematically destroyed. The Catholic Youth groups were molested at first only by the Hitler Youth, but in 1935 they were forbidden by law to engage in any sport, or social or educational activity. Civil servants were required to enlist their children in the Hitler Youth or lose their posts in the government. After 1937, enlistment in the Hitler Youth was compulsory for all children, and membership in both organizations was forbidden.

Karl Barth spoke with authority for religion in postwar Germany: "Freedom is the gift of God, but man must exercise it." The chief problem facing the German churches was to revive the interest, recapture the confidence, and re-enlist the participation of the masses in church work. The majority of Germans turn to the church for only four things—baptism, confirmation, marriage, and burial—leaving it out of their everyday lives. Perhaps the ecclesiastical organization has too few devoted volunteer church workers, and certainly it has too few pastors. The average pastoral charge has nearly three thousand parishioners, and one parish of twenty-two thousand has only two ministers.

The problem is complicated in East Germany by government opposition. Communist state programs, often involving compulsory attendance, are timed to coincide with church functions. Salaries of clergy are meager. Organized propaganda is designed to discredit pastors with their flock.

There is also great need for internal unity among the church bodies. The EKID (Evangelische Kirche in Deutschland) was an organization of German churches set up during the Hitler regime as a fighting unit without theological foundations, with a membership of thirteen Lutheran, one Reformed, and thirteen Evangelical bodies. While this organization is an attempt at uniform action, it expends much energy that could be better used for the solution of the primary problem cited above.

The restoration of a sane, well-balanced religious life

in Germany is one of the great internal German problems to be faced in our time.

U.S.S.R.

Marx opposed religion on the ground that it supported the idea of private property. His saying that "religion is the opium of the people" was adopted by Lenin, and we find the latter requiring that all Communist leaders renounce religion. All the churches were closed and the chapels destroyed following the Revolution. Most of the property of the Russian Orthodox Church was confiscated, including more than six hundred of the thousand monasteries and convents, the sacred vessels and vestments, all the real estate, the ikons, and the hoard of Church treasure estimated at one and a half billion dollars. The priests were deprived of all control over education, marriage, divorce, and registration of births and deaths. Resistance led to arrest, and some of those who were arrested were executed by firing squad. Religious services were discouraged, but allowed under permit where the priest could live on voluntary contributions. All government grants and church subsidies were stopped. The Soviet government sought to ridicule religion through burlesque satires on religious subjects. The press opened a campaign against it, with two magazines motivated entirely by this object. Education was directed toward the same end. A "Society of the Militant Godless" was organized.

Hostility to religion and suppression of it led to much criticism of the Soviet from outside sources. After 1929, under direction of Joseph Stalin, there was a change in policy. The people were permitted to hold any religious belief, but the activities of the church were confined to purely religious pursuits—no charitable or educational work being allowed. The census of 1937 showed that still one-third of the urban and two-thirds of the rural population in the Soviet Union was Christian.

This last fact was largely due to the work of a single man, Sergei, who was willing to make salvation of souls the single purpose of the church and to leave education and politics to other bodies. Stalin was a realist, and in 1943 he had the Russian Orthodox Church restored with Sergei as Patriarch. Stalin realized that such a restoration was the equivalent of religious occupation of a great part of southeastern Europe, for Moscow is now the religious capital for an estimated one hundred million Christians.

At the time of the restoration of the Church, the Society of the Militant Godless was disbanded, and both of the antireligious magazines mentioned above were suspended. The Bible is being printed again in Russia for the first time since the 1917 Revolution. A new seminary is being opened in Moscow for the training of men for the priesthood. The movement has every appearance of permanence.

Although the party line is still antireligious, there is a resurgence of religious belief among the common people. Many peasants had their children baptized surreptitiously; now they turn to the churches openly for baptism, marriage, and burial. Most of the old churches have been re-opened, many new ones have been built, and about a dozen seminaries are in operation. The state realized the use and value of the church during the war; as a result the official position is defined as one of taking no overt action against the church or clergy, but of trying to influence by example and teaching. After Stalin's death, there was marked improvement in the position of the clergy. High-ranking churchmen are present at important state functions and are placed in the official press lists between the top politicos and the heads of the party propaganda committees. The official report of the National Council of Churches' delegation to Russia in 1956 read in part, "It is apparent that the church and state have reached at least a temporary accommodation. . . . Congregations were large and devout. . . . Enrollment in theological seminaries [was] at capacity. . . . The churches [were] confined within themselves . . . little concern for social or intellectual life. . . ."

"Life is short; the Volga is long; man's need for religion is eternal."

Index

Aaron, 15
Abraham, 32
absolution, 27
Abydos, 9
Acropolis, 17
Act of Supremacy, 101
Act of Toleration, 105
Adonis, 18
Aeneas, 19
Aesculapius, 17
Affair, The, 37, 39
Ahriman, 36
Ahura Mazda, 36
Alexius, 97
Amenhotep (see Ikhnaton)
Amon, 8
Amos, 33
Analects, 52
Ananda, 46
ancestor worship, 8, 50
anchorites, 41, 90
animal worship, 8
Anu, 12
Aphrodite, 18
Apollo, 17
Apostles' Creed, 78
Apostolic succession, 79
Aquinas, Thomas, 93
Arahatship, 44
Aristotle, 35, 55
Arius, Arianism, 78
Armaiti, 36
Artemis, 17
Arunta, 3
Asgard, 22
Ashtoreth, 12
Assur, 12, 14
Astarte, 12
Athanasian Creed, 73, 78
Athanasius, 77, 90

Athena, 17
Aton, 10
Attis, 19, 20
Augsburg Confession, 102, 11
Augustine, 73, 74, 77, 90
Avesta, 37
Avignon, 87
Aztecs, 15, 24 ff.

Bahá'i, 126
Balder, 9, 22
baptism, 28, 30, 76, 126
Baptists, 104
Bel, Bel-Marduk, 7, 12, 13
Beltane, 6
Beltis, 12
Benedictine Rule, 90
Bhagavad-Gita, 42
Bismarck, 103
Black Friday, 20, 57
Boniface, 87
Book of Common Prayer, 101
Book of the Dead, 9, 10
Book of Mormon, 122
Book of Recompense, 50
Brahma, 15, 40
Buddha, Buddhism, 43 ff.
burial rites, 5, 9, 10, 16, 27, 29

Calvin, John, 102, 115 f.
canon law, 75
Cassian, John, 90
Cathari, 79
Catholic Emancipation Act, 105
Catholic Youth, 130
celibacy, 26, 91
Celt, Celtic, 5 f.
Cerberus, 55
Ceres, 19
charity, 28, 66, 81

133